Montgomery County-Norristown
Public Library

This project is made possible
through a grant from the Institute of Museum
and Library Services as administered by
Pennsylvania Department of Education
and the Commonwealth of Pennsylvania,
Tom Corbett, Governor

UNDERSTANDING DRUGS

DRUGS

Morphine

TITLES IN THE *UNDERSTANDING DRUGS* SERIES

UNDERSTANDING DRUGS

Morphine

M. FOSTER OLIVE, PH.D.

CONSULTING EDITOR
DAVID J. TRIGGLE, PH.D.
University Professor
School of Pharmacy and Pharmaceutical Sciences
State University of New York at Buffalo

CHELSEA HOUSE
An Infobase Learning Company

Chelsea House
An imprint of Infobase Learning
132 West 31st Street
New York NY 10001

Library of Congress Cataloging-in-Publication Data

Olive, M. Foster.
   Morphine / M. Foster Olive ; consulting editor David J. Triggle.
     p. cm. — (Understanding drugs)
   Includes bibliographical references and index.
   ISBN-13: 978-1-60413-544-2 (hardcover : alk. paper)
   ISBN-10: 1-60413-544-1 (hardcover : alk. paper)   1. Morphine—Juvenile
    literature.   2. Opium—Juvenile literature.   I. Title.   II. Series.
   RM666.M8O45   2011
   362.29'3—dc22
                                         2010035763

Chelsea House books are available at special discounts when purchased in bulk quantities for businesses, associations, institutions, or sales promotions. Please call our Special Sales Department in New York at (212) 967-8800 or (800) 322-8755.

You can find Chelsea House on the World Wide Web at
http://www.chelseahouse.com

Text design by Kerry Casey
Cover design by Alicia Post
Composition by Newgen
Cover printed by Bang Printing, Brainerd, Minn.
Book printed and bound by Bang Printing, Brainerd, Minn.
Date printed: January 2011
Printed in the United States of America

10 9 8 7 6 5 4 3 2 1

This book is printed on acid-free paper.

All links and Web addresses were checked and verified to be correct at the time of publication. Because of the dynamic nature of the Web, some addresses and links may have changed since publication and may no longer be valid.

Contents

foreword

THE USE AND ABUSE OF DRUGS

For thousands of years, humans have used a variety of sources with which to cure their ills, cast out devils, promote their well-being, relieve their misery, and control their fertility. Until the beginning of the twentieth century, the agents used were all of natural origin, including many derived from plants as well as elements such as antimony, sulfur, mercury, and arsenic. The sixteenth-century alchemist and physician Paracelsus used mercury and arsenic in his treatment of syphilis, worms, and other diseases that were common at that time; his cure rates, however, remain unknown. Many drugs used today have their origins in natural products. Antimony derivatives, for example, are used in the treatment of the nasty tropical disease leishmaniasis. These plant-derived products represent molecules that have been "forged in the crucible of evolution" and continue to supply the scientist with molecular scaffolds for new drug development.

Our story of modern drug discovery may be considered to start with the German physician and scientist Paul Ehrlich, often called the father of chemotherapy. Born in 1854, Ehrlich became interested in the ways in which synthetic dyes, then becoming a major product of the German fine chemical industry, could selectively stain certain tissues and components of cells. He reasoned that such dyes might form the basis for drugs that could interact selectively with diseased or foreign cells and organisms. One of Ehrlich's early successes was development of the arsenical "606"—patented under the name *Salvarsan*—as a treatment for syphilis. Ehrlich's goal was to create a "magic bullet," a drug that would target only the diseased cell or the invading disease-causing organism and have no effect on healthy cells and tissues. In this he was not successful, but his great research did lay the groundwork for the successes of the twentieth century, including the discovery of the sulfonamides and the antibiotic penicillin. The latter agent saved countless lives during World War II. Ehrlich, like many scientists, was an optimist. On the eve of World War I, he wrote, "Now that the liability to, and danger of, disease are to a large extent circumscribed—the efforts of chemotherapeutics are directed as far as possible to fill up the gaps left in this ring." As we shall see in the pages of this volume, it is neither the first nor the last time that science has proclaimed its victory over nature, only to have to see this optimism dashed in the light of some freshly emerging infection.

From these advances, however, has come the vast array of drugs that are available to the modern physician. We are increasingly close to Ehrlich's magic bullet: Drugs can now target very specific molecular defects in a number of cancers, and doctors today have the ability to investigate the human genome to more effectively match the drug and the patient. In the next one to two decades, it is almost certain that the cost of "reading" an individual genome will be sufficiently cheap that, at least in the developed world, such personalized medicines will become the norm. The development of such drugs, however, is extremely costly and raises significant social issues, including equity in the delivery of medical treatment.

The twenty-first century will continue to produce major advances in medicines and medicine delivery. Nature is, however, a resilient foe. Diseases and organisms develop resistance to existing drugs, and new drugs must constantly be developed. (This is particularly true for anti-infective and anticancer agents.) Additionally, new and more lethal forms of existing infectious diseases can develop rapidly. With the ease of global travel, these can spread from Timbuktu to Toledo in less than 24 hours and become pandemics. Hence the current concerns with avian flu. Also, diseases that have previously been dormant or geographically circumscribed may suddenly break out worldwide. (Imagine, for example, a worldwide pandemic of Ebola disease, with public health agencies totally overwhelmed.) Finally, there are serious concerns regarding the possibility of man-made epidemics occurring through the deliberate or accidental spread of disease agents—including manufactured agents, such as smallpox with enhanced lethality. It is therefore imperative that the search for new medicines continue.

All of us at some time in our life will take a medicine, even if it is only aspirin for a headache or to reduce cosmetic defects. For some individuals, drug use will be constant throughout life. As we age, we will likely be exposed to a variety of medications—from childhood vaccines to drugs to relieve pain caused by a terminal disease. It is not easy to get accurate and understandable information about the drugs that we consume to treat diseases and disorders. There are, of course, highly specialized volumes aimed at medical or scientific professionals. These, however, demand a sophisticated knowledge base and experience to be comprehended. Advertising on television is widely available but provides only fleeting information, usually about only a single drug and designed to market rather than inform. The intent of this series of books, **Understanding Drugs**, is to provide the lay reader with intelligent, readable, and accurate descriptions of drugs, why and how they are used, their limitations, their side effects, and their future. The series will discuss both *"treatment drugs"*—typically, but not exclusively, prescription drugs, that have well-established criteria of both efficacy and safety—and *"drugs of abuse,"* agents that have pronounced pharmacological and physiological effects but that are, for a variety of reasons, not to be considered for therapeutic purposes. It is our hope that these books will provide readers with sufficient information to satisfy their immediate needs and to serve as an adequate base for further investigation and for asking intelligent questions of health care providers.

—David J. Triggle, Ph.D.
University Professor
School of Pharmacy and Pharmaceutical Sciences
State University of New York at Buffalo

Overview of Morphine

One day, while on foot patrol in Baghdad as a part of Operation Iraqi Freedom, Private First Class John Morse was wounded when a car bomb exploded approximately 25 yards from him. The force of the explosion knocked Private Morse to the ground, and also sent a shard of metal the size of a dinner plate flying through the air directly towards him. The piece of metal struck him in the upper thigh, tearing through his fatigues and penetrating approximately two inches into his flesh. After lying in a daze for a few minutes, Private Morse suddenly began to feel excruciating pain coming from his leg wound. He shouted out for a medic, and fortunately the platoon's medic was about 50 yards farther away from the blast than Private Morse and was unhurt by the explosion. Hearing his call for help, the medic immediately rushed to Private Morse's aid. After assessing his fellow soldier's wound and noting that the amount of bleeding was not excessive, the medic felt that removing the shard of metal from Private Morse's leg there in the middle of the street would cause him a tremendous amount of pain and might actually sever his femoral artery, potentially causing Private Morse to bleed to death. To relieve Private Morse's pain, the medic administered him a dose of morphine from a prepared syringe that he carried in a pouch along with other medical supplies. The medic then signaled to several other soldiers to assist him in placing Private Morse on a stretcher (with the metal shard still in his leg) and carrying him approximately a quarter of a mile back to the platoon's station. By the time they got there, Private Morse was heavily sedated and felt only slight pain from his

9

wound. Private Morse's eyelids felt heavy and his thoughts and speech were slowed. Within 10 minutes, a medical helicopter had arrived to airlift Private Morse to a military hospital located several miles away. It was there that Private Morse was placed under general anesthesia and the metal shard was surgically removed from his leg, and the damaged muscle and skin were sutured closed. In the recovery area of the hospital, Private Morse was implanted with an intravenous catheter in his forearm that slowly dripped a morphine solution into his vein. By his second day of recovery, Private Morse was feeling less drowsy and also found that the morphine was losing its ability to relieve the pain from his wound. After he notified the medical assistant of his increased pain levels, his intravenous catheter was removed and Private Morse was instructed to take a stronger dose of a different pain reliever called oxycodone three times a day in tablet form. Over the next several weeks, the medical staff slowly lowered Private Morse's dosage of oxycodone. Eventually, as his wound healed, Private Morse found that he could control his pain levels with nonprescription pain relievers such as ibuprofen.

WHAT IS MORPHINE?

Morphine is one of the oldest and most powerful pain relievers, or **analgesics**, to be discovered. It is called an **opiate** drug because morphine is one of the main chemicals found in **opium**, a gooey, saplike substance obtained from the opium poppy, *Papaver somniferum* (see Figure 1.1). The word opium is derived from the Greek word for poppy juice, *opos*.[1] The opium poppy grows naturally in southeastern Europe and Asia in countries such as Iran, Turkey, Pakistan, Afghanistan, India, Laos, Burma (Myanmar), and Vietnam. The opium poppy is also grown and harvested in Central and South American countries such as Guatemala, Colombia, and Mexico, as well as on the continent of Australia. Opium poppies are grown primarily for the illegal production of the highly addictive drug heroin, which is derived from the morphine contained in opium.

Drawing and writings referring to the use of opium have been found that date back to approximately 5000 B.C. Archeological tablets dating back

Figure 1.1 The opium poppy *Papaver somniferum*. *(© Jerry Mason/ Photo Researchers, Inc.)*

to 3500 B.C. that were written by the ancient Mesopotamians in southwest Asia refer to the opium poppy as "Hul Gil" (which means "joy plant"). During the sixteenth century, a noted English **apothecary** (an ancient term for a pharmacist) named Thomas Sydenham wrote that of the "remedies which it has pleased Almighty God to give to man to relieve his sufferings, none is so universal and so efficacious as opium."[2] Morphine as one of the main analgesic components of opium was not identified until the early eighteenth century. More detailed information on the history of opium and morphine can be found in Chapter 2.

Morphine is just one of many pain-relieving and pleasurable chemicals found in opium poppies. More than 30 different morphine-like chemicals, including codeine, can be found in raw opium, as will be discussed in Chapter 3. However, morphine is the most abundant of these chemicals found in opium.

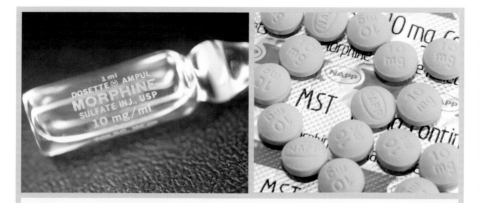

Figure 1.2 Morphine is often packaged in small glass vials called ampules and administered in a hospital setting or doctor's office with a hypodermic syringe into the skin, muscle, or vein. When prescribed as a pain reliever for patients to take at home, morphine is given in pill form. *(© Scott Camazine/ Photo Researchers, Inc./ © Paul Mogford/ Alamy)*

Morphine can produce extraordinary relief from many types of pain, but also produces other effects such as sedation, constipation, lowered pulse and blood pressure, and feelings of extreme pleasure (called **euphoria**). Chapter 4 will provide more detail on the psychological and biological effects of morphine and related drugs. Morphine and other opiate drugs are often called **narcotic** drugs, since in high doses they can produce heavy sedation and a sleep- or coma-like state called **narcosis**. In fact, morphine was named after Morpheus, the Greek god of dreams, due to its ability to produce heavy sedation and **stupor**.

Today, there are literally dozens of narcotic pain relievers that have a chemical structure similar to that of morphine. These drugs as often referred to as opiate **alkaloids**. Alkaloids are naturally occurring chemical compounds that contain nitrogen atoms and, when dissolved into water or other liquids, cause the solution to have an **alkaline** pH (a common index of whether a chemical is acidic, corrosive, basic, alkaline, or neutral). Commonly prescribed narcotic analgesics include codeine, oxycodone (Percocet, Percodan, or Oxycontin), hydrocodone (Lortab or Vicodin), hydromorphone (Dilaudid), meperidine (Demerol), propoxyphene (Darvon), fentanyl (Sublimaze), fentanyl derivatives such as alfentanil (Alfenta) and sufentanil (Sufenta), and tramadol (Ultram). These drugs, which are discussed in more detail in Chapter 5, are commonly used as prescription pain relievers in the form of a pill, but can also be administered to the patient intravenously or directly into the spinal fluid (called an **epidural**, usually performed during childbirth).

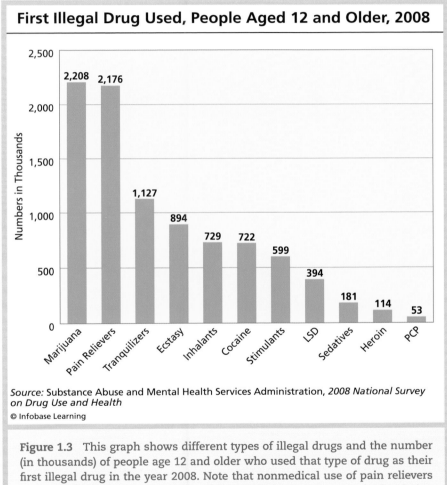

First Illegal Drug Used, People Aged 12 and Older, 2008

Source: Substance Abuse and Mental Health Services Administration, *2008 National Survey on Drug Use and Health*
© Infobase Learning

Figure 1.3 This graph shows different types of illegal drugs and the number (in thousands) of people age 12 and older who used that type of drug as their first illegal drug in the year 2008. Note that nonmedical use of pain relievers is the second most common form of first used illegal drug, with the first being marijuana.

Because morphine and other narcotic pain relievers are usually taken for severe pain conditions that require numerous days of medication, prolonged use of these narcotics can result in dependence and addiction, even when the pain that necessitated a prescription for the narcotic has disappeared. The use of prescription narcotic pain relievers for reasons other than pain relief is termed **nonmedical use**, and is a growing problem in the United States and elsewhere. Opiate narcotics, including morphine, are the primary type of prescription pain reliever that is addictive and habit-forming. The 2008 National Survey on Drug Use and Health found that during the time period

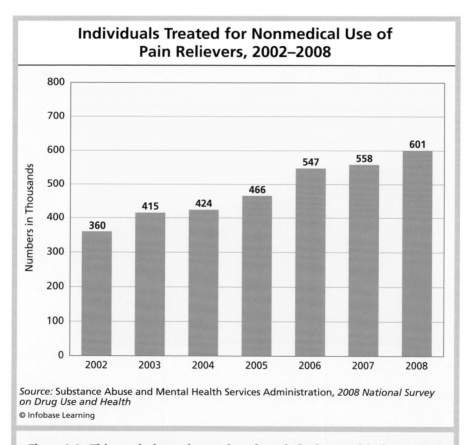

Individuals Treated for Nonmedical Use of Pain Relievers, 2002–2008

Source: Substance Abuse and Mental Health Services Administration, *2008 National Survey on Drug Use and Health*

© Infobase Learning

Figure 1.4 This graph shows the number of people (in thousands) who received treatment for nonmedical use of pain relievers during the years 2002–08. This demonstrates the growing number of people who are becoming addicted to and seek help for nonmedical use of prescription pain relievers.

2002–08, the rate of nonmedical use of prescription pain relievers among young adults aged 18 to 25 increased from 4.1 percent in 2002 to 4.6 percent in 2008.[3] During this time period, the number of people who sought treatment for addiction to prescription pain relievers almost doubled (see Figure 1.4). In fact, during 2008, among first-time users, prescription pain relievers were the second most popular drug used illegally (marijuana was first). (See Figure 1.3.)

MORPHINE IS A HEROIN PRECURSOR AND METABOLITE

As discussed earlier, morphine is the most abundant chemical found in opium, and opium poppies are grown primarily for the production of the highly addictive and illegal opiate drug heroin. It turns out that there is an interesting reciprocal relationship between morphine and heroin. When injected into the bloodstream, morphine penetrates the brain at a rate much slower than that of heroin. This is due to the different chemical structures of morphine and heroin (the chemical name for heroin is, in fact, diacetylmorphine). The chemical structure of heroin allows it to pass from blood vessels in the brain into the tissue of the brain itself much faster than morphine. The blood vessels of the brain are unique to those compared to the rest of the body as their walls are impermeable to many substances that are ordinarily permeable in blood vessels in other parts of the body. This impermeability of the brain's blood vessel walls makes up what is known as the **blood-brain barrier**, or BBB. The ability of heroin to pass through the BBB more easily than morphine is believed to be the reason why heroin produces a much more intense "rush" and euphoria than that produced by morphine. Once inside the brain, however, heroin is rapidly converted back to morphine, and ultimately morphine is metabolized by the liver. In other words, heroin is essentially a vehicle for morphine to rapidly penetrate into the brain and produce a much more intense euphoria than morphine itself. Despite the faster penetration of heroin into the brain as compared to morphine, morphine is still an addictive substance.

Like all addictive drugs, morphine has been given various slang terms. These include M, Miss Emma, monkey, morph, duramorph, Murphy, Roxane (a common brand name of prescription morphine), or white stuff (after its appearance in chemical form).[4] Morphine and related narcotic drugs pose numerous potential problems to the user, including the development of **tolerance** (diminished effectiveness of the drug when used for extended periods of time), unwanted side effects (such as itching, abdominal cramping, constipation, nausea, vomiting, and immune system problems), nonmedical use and abuse, the potential for fatal overdose, the potential for the drug to become habit-forming or addictive, and severely unpleasant **withdrawal** symptoms when their use is discontinued. Most people who become addicted to morphine or other opiates usually require professional psychological and/or medical help and intervention to overcome their addiction.

One of the most common medical treatments for opiate addiction is the use of **maintenance therapy** (sometimes called **replacement therapy**), in which long-acting, less potent, and less dangerous opiate drugs such as methadone (Dolophine) and buprenorphine (Buprenex or Suboxone) are given to mimic the effects of problematic opiates such as morphine or heroin in the body. So, when an addict is attempting to stop using heroin or morphine, he or she can avoid the extreme discomfort of opiate withdrawal by taking methadone or buprenorphine. If the addict avoids relapsing to the use of morphine or heroin, he or she can be "weaned off" or have the dose of methadone or buprenorphine slowly tapered off over a period of many weeks, and eventually become opiate free. This type of replacement therapy is similar to the way nicotine patches deliver nicotine to the body and are used to help people stop cigarette smoking. Other drugs, such as naloxone or naltrexone, which prevent opiates from exerting their effects on the nervous system, are also often used to treat opiate addiction. Organizations such as Narcotics Anonymous (commonly referred to as NA) provide group support therapy and offer resources for addicts and their friends or relatives who have been affected by the addict's problematic use of opiates.

2

History of Morphine

The use of opium by humans for medicinal or recreational purposes dates back thousands of years. It is even mentioned in one of the most famous poems of all time, Homer's Odyssey, *written in the eighth century* B.C. *The main character, Odysseus, has gone to the city of Troy to fight in the Trojan War, and is absent from his wife, Penelope, his son Telemachus, and their many friends for a number of years. To soothe their grief, the Greek goddess Helen, daughter of Zeus, the king of the gods, gives Telemachus and his friends a some drugged wine. Homer writes, "She cast a drug into the wine of which they drank to lull all pain and anger and bring forgetfulness of every sorrow." Although opium is not mentioned specifically as the drug that Helen added to the wine (the drug was actually referred to as "Nepenthes pharmakon," which translates to "a drug that chases away sorrow"), most historians and modern pharmacologists believe the drug was in fact opium. There are, however, skeptics who believe the drug that was added to the wine was an extract of the henbane plant, which contains a well-known chemical called scopolamine that can cause amnesia.[1] However, henbane is a very toxic plant, and ingestion of even small quantities of it can be fatal in humans and other animals. Because Homer does not write of such toxic effects of the wine in the* Odyssey, *many pharmacologists interpret this as confirmation of their theory that the drug was indeed opium. Today, in some parts of the Middle East, teas made with opium are still served at funerals to ease the grief of the bereaved.*

Morphine was not identified as one of the primary analgesic and pleasurable chemicals in the opium poppy until the eighteenth century. However, the history of opium use dates back many thousands of years. Before discussing the history of morphine use, a history of the cultivation, trafficking, and use of opium will first be given.

THE HISTORY OF OPIUM

Although it is impossible to precisely determine who first discovered the potent pain relieving and pleasurable effects of opium, some of the earliest writings about it were by ancient Sumerians, circa 4000 B.C. These people, who lived the southwestern portion of Asia in what is now known as Iraq, termed the opium poppy *hul gil*, which means "joy plant."[2]. The plant was also known to exist in Europe at least 4,000 years ago as evidenced by fossil remains of poppy pods and seeds found in Switzerland. Opium was grown, cultivated, and used by many ancient empires, including the Sumerian, Assyrian, Egyptian, Minoan, Greek, Roman, Persian, and Arab empires. During these ancient times, opium was the most potent form of pain relief available, and it allowed ancient doctors and other healers to perform prolonged surgical procedures. Opium is mentioned in many important medical texts of the ancient world. One of these is the Ebers Papyrus, in which opium is advocated as a remedy to stop children from crying (probably due to its ability to relieve teething pain, as well as produce sedation). Noted ancient Greek physician Hippocrates (460–357 B.C.) prescribed drinking the juice of the opium poppy mixed with the seed of the nettle plant. Other noteworthy users of opium were Alexander the Great, who introduced opium to the people of Persia and India around 300 B.C., and Marcus Aurelius, emperor of Rome, who took opium to sleep and to cope with the difficulty of military campaigns.[3] A noted Arab philosopher and physician by the name of Abu-Ali-Ibn-Sina (Avicenna), who lived around the turn of the first millennium A.D., proposed opium as a remedy for diarrhea, diseases of the eyes, and to help people sleep.

The opium poppy was introduced to China in approximately the fourth century A.D. by Arab traders who advocated its use for medicinal purposes. However, in Chinese literature, there are earlier references to its use. The noted Chinese surgeon Hua To of the Three Kingdoms (A.D. 220–264) had his patients swallow opium preparations and *Cannabis indica* before undergoing major surgery. Regardless, by the turn of the first millennium A.D., the use of opium in China was widespread, from the common household where it was used as a remedy for aches and pains, to the military, which believed it would increase courage, to rulers who indulged.

During the thirteenth century, opium largely disappeared from Europe because of the Holy Inquisition, an attempt by the Roman Catholic Church to "purify" the entire continent through torture or execution of nonbelievers or heretics (people who were deemed not to abide by the rules of the church). The use of opium was considered a form of heresy because it was tied to Eastern religions.

By the fifteenth century, opium had been introduced to India and its use became widespread. The first dynasty of Moghul rulers was founded during this time, and they capitalized on the profits of opium poppy cultivation and trade, and established a state monopoly on the sale of opium. Around this same time period, opium was reintroduced into European medical literature as **laudanum**, which consisted of opium mixed with citrus juice or alcohol. The most popular commercial brand was Sydenham's Laudanum, which was introduced in 1527 and consisted of one pound sherry wine, two ounces of opium, and one ounce each of saffron, cinnamon powder, and clove powder.

CHINA AND THE OPIUM WARS

The opium trade continued to spread to other regions of the world, including Central and South America, but China remained the epicenter of the world's opium trade. In the sixteenth century, China's increasing population and bounty of arable land (land suitable for farming) greatly reduced trade with Western countries, as China had little need for Western goods. However, Western countries sought trade with China for its precious tea and silk. An equal trading commodity was desperately needed, and opium proved to be the perfect medium of exchange, as it was highly addictive and could grow in many climates around the world. Portugal was the first country to establish and capitalize on opium trade with China. Initially trading tobacco from their Brazilian colony, the Portuguese, followed by many other European nations, quickly realized opium was a better medium of trade than tobacco. Particularly eager to enter the opium trade were Dutch merchants who, like the Portuguese, hoped to monopolize the Chinese opium trade. Through the Dutch East India Company, they were able to extensively expand their trade holdings by securing monopolies in India. By the late 1600s India was providing the Dutch with large quantities of cheap opium that they were able to sell to China at a substantial profit. The resulting mass addiction to opium by the Chinese pressured the emperor to place the first ban on opium in 1729. However, the opium trade continued because of the large income it generated.

By 1773, India was colonized by Britain, and through the established British East India Company, the British were able to topple the Dutch monopoly over the opium trade with China, eventually making the Bengal region of India the world's capital of opium production. As Bengal had its own massive supply of opium, the Bengalese governor made it illegal to ship opium to rival China. To bypass this shipping ban, opium produced in Bengal was sold to private British merchants who transported opium into China on their personal vessels. This allowed opium sales to China to steadily increase during the next century. Since India and its provinces, including Bengal, were still under British control, the British government ousted all local opium buyers in 1797 and became the predominant worldwide exporter of opium, a status that lasted throughout the nineteenth century.

The competition between China and British-ruled India for the trade of opium caused great tension. With the number of opium addicts in China increasing exponentially, the Chinese government began to enforce strict punishment for using opium, including imprisonment and, in some cases, death. These efforts at curtailing opium use turned out to be futile, and trade continued to thrive in China as customs officials were bribed to allow opium to continue across the border. The Qing emperor of China continued his efforts to thwart the opium trade by writing Queen Victoria of England a letter pleading with her to stop the trade and end the bitterness it created between the two governments. It is unknown whether the queen received the letter, read it, or dismissed it altogether, but the opium trade continued and tensions continued to rise.

With no response from the queen, the Qing emperor was even more determined to shut down the opium trade. In 1839, he blocked access to the main Chinese port of Canton, where a high volume of opium was being imported, which trapped more than 300 British traders in the city. The British traders were forced to either forfeit their opium supply or face execution.

Figure 2.1 When the raw opium sap is collected and allowed to dry, it crystal-lizes. Certain chemical processing procedures cause the opium to turn into a thick, gooey black substance called black tar opium. Morphine can be purified from both of these types of opium and converted to heroin by relatively simple chemical procedures. *(Drug Enforcement Administration)*

In retaliation, the British declared war and attacked the port of Canton in November 1839.

The First Opium War ended quickly with British forces defeating China and forcing the country to sign the Treaty of Nanjing in 1842, in which Brit-ain agreed to formally discourage opium smuggling, but also forced China to open five additional ports to the British. In addition, China was required to pay Britain 4.5 million pounds for the losses of opium, soldiers, and British vessels that had occurred during the war. Britain was also allowed control of the island of Hong Kong, which it used to store opium for sale on the Chinese mainland. For the next 15 years, tensions between Britain and China sim-mered, and in 1857 a second war was declared.

The Second Opium War proved to be more vicious than the first. In one of the first battles, more than 10,000 Chinese were captured and killed in the port of Canton. Just 27 hours into the war, Canton was in flames and more than 30,000 homes had been burned. Although it seemed that Britain again held the upper hand in this war, the Chinese government refused to sign a new treaty. In response to the Chinese defiance, British forces invaded Peking, the Chinese capital. To avoid a repeat of the destruction that occurred in Canton, the Chinese government signed the Treaty of Tientsin in 1858. This treaty legalized the sale and use of opium in China, and with opium now a legal global commodity, opium addiction began to spread worldwide and the continued trade of opium caused numerous national economies also to be dependent on the trade of opium.

OPIUM COMES TO AMERICA

Around the time of the end of the Second Opium War, the United States was increasingly becoming the land of prosperity and the "American dream" was attracting many to the young country. Industrialization was a major player in the success of America, with new industries requiring a larger workforce. In addition, the California Gold Rush, with its chance of unbridled wealth, had American frontiersmen swarming to the West Coast. This migration only added to growth of the country, with additional major demands arising from the expansion of the railroad industry. This massive industrialization of the United States caused a significant labor shortage. As a result, numerous impoverished Chinese looking for work and the promise of a better life immigrated to America. They referred to the United States as the "Golden Mountain." Tens of thousands of Chinese immigrant workers found no shortage of employment opportunities in California and claimed it as their new home.

However, Chinese immigrants brought not only their labor but their opium addiction as well. Though the Chinese are often blamed for the introduction of opium to America, opium was already used throughout the United States as pharmaceutical companies attempted to develop formulations of opium for the treatment of pain and other medical conditions. Since opium was still legal in the United States, business owners tolerated its use—and, in some cases, they used it as a way to control and bribe addicted Chinese immigrants. These immigrants were often treated poorly in other ways as well, and their immigration to the United States was met with resistance from U.S. citizens. Eventually, anti-Chinese racism forced them to live within confined areas called Chinatowns within larger metropolitan areas. In these Chinatowns, **opium dens** (where people went to buy and smoke opium and become sedated) began to appear.

THE DISCOVERY OF MORPHINE

About 50 years prior to the end of the Opium Wars, in 1806–07, a German pharmacist named Friedrich Wilhelm Adam Sertürner (Figure 2.2) reported the isolation of morphine as one of the primary components of opium.[4] He named the chemical "morphium" after the Greek god of dreams, Morpheus. The name "morphium" eventually evolved into "morphine." Not only was morphine the first individual chemical to be extracted from opium, but it was also the first alkaloid substance to be isolated from any plant for medicinal purposes. After the discovery of morphine, scientists and chemists further investigated the chemical properties of morphine, and found it was much more stable, effective, and able to be dissolved in water or saline (so it could be injected) if it were combined with the chemical sulfate. Thus, morphine sulfate became, and continues to be, the most widely used form of morphine.

The isolation of morphine from raw opium by Sertürner was followed by isolation of other analgesic alkaloids found in opium, including codeine in 1832, thebaine in 1835, and papaverine in 1848. During the 1850s, doctors commonly prescribed purified formulations of these opiate alkaloids, rather than raw opium, for the relief of pain, cough, and diarrhea. This same time period also witnessed the development of the hypodermic syringe, which allowed doctors to inject morphine or other opiate alkaloids directly into the bloodstream or muscle tissue, delivering faster pain relief than that provided by pill or powder form.

The development of morphine in an injectable form in the 1850s came at a rather fortuitous time, since the American Civil War erupted during the following decade (1861–65). Morphine provided fast and potent pain relief for Civil War soldiers wounded on the battlefield. Throughout the war, millions of opium pills and tens of thousands of ounces of morphine sulfate were issued by military doctors and medics. Unfortunately, however, an estimated 100,000 Civil War soldiers became addicted to morphine, and morphine addiction was often called the "army disease" or "soldier's disease."

Figure 2.2 German pharmacist Friedrich Wilhelm Adam Sertürner (1783–1841), discoverer of morphine. *(© Hulton Archive/ Getty Images)*

THE RISE OF HEROIN

The mass addiction to opium and morphine produced by its widespread administration during the Civil War prompted pharmacists and scientists to seek out pain relievers that were just as effective and potent as morphine or opium, but were not addictive. In the 1870s, chemists produced a form of morphine called 3,6-diacetylmorphine, which was first sold in 1898 by the German pharmaceutical company Bayer under the brand name of Heroin. It was an effective cough suppressant and antidiarrheal medication, but not too long after the turn of the twentieth century it became evident that Heroin was a dangerous and highly addictive drug.

The highly addictive nature of heroin and the fatal overdoses it often produced sparked a worldwide effort to control the growing, manufacturing and distribution of opium and the numerous problems it caused. In 1909, the first meeting of International Opium Commission was held, attended by representatives from 13 countries. The Netherlands was host to the second meeting of the International Opium Commission in 1911, which pressured all nations to establish domestic opium laws. Unfortunately, however, independent nations were at liberty to ignore the advised policies, and again international efforts failed to curb the opium trade.

In response to the threat posed by heroin and other opiates, the United States Congress passed the Harrison Narcotics Act in December 1914, which enacted governmental control of each phase of the preparation and distribution of medicinal opium, morphine, heroin, and any other opiate derivative that had similar addictive properties. It also criminalized the possession of opiates.

World Wars I and II drew attention away from the heroin and opium trade during the 1920s through 1950s, although the development of other opiate pain relievers such as meperidine (1939) and methadone (1946) continued during this time. During the latter half of the 1960s, the first large-scale smuggling of heroin into the United States took place: Turkish opium was exported to France for processing into heroin, which was then smuggled into New York City. In the 1970s, a brand of heroin dubbed "Mexican brown" heroin became available as a cheaper alternative to European heroin. In the

(*continues on page 28*)

OPIUM, AFGHANISTAN, AND THE TALIBAN

The supply of heroin from the southwestern Asian country of Afghanistan was disrupted following the 1979 invasion by the Soviet Union and its subsequent occupation of this country for 10 years. When the Russians exited Afghanistan in 1988–89, Afghani warlords began to

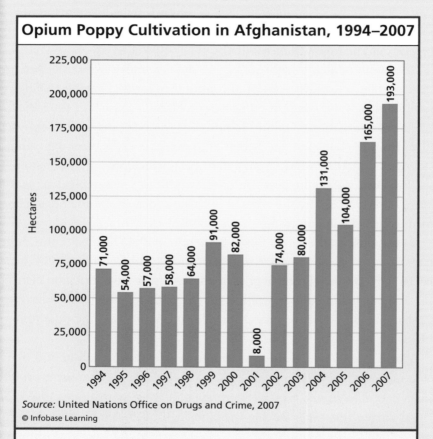

Opium Poppy Cultivation in Afghanistan, 1994–2007

Source: United Nations Office on Drugs and Crime, 2007

© Infobase Learning

Figure 2.3. Opium poppy cultivation in Afghanistan during the years 1994 to 2007, expressed in hectares (1 hectare = 2.47 acres). Notice the tremendous drop in cultivation in 2001, a result of the Taliban outlawing opium production in 2000. Opium farming resumed immediately following the ouster of the Taliban from power by U.S.–led military forces in the wake of the September 11, 2001, terrorist attacks.

control much of the country's production of opium. In 1996, the Taliban seized power in Afghanistan, and in 2000 outlawed the cultivation and use of the drug, reducing the opium production by more than 90 percent (see Figure 2.3). This setback in opium production was short-lived, as the Taliban were removed from power by U.S.–led forces in retaliation for the terrorist attacks of September 11, 2001. When Taliban control of Afghanistan ended, so did the ban on opium production. Today the country provides between 75 and 85 percent of the world's opium supply.

While it might seem simple for the new Afghani government to again outlaw opium production and eradicate opium poppy fields, for many farmers in Afghanistan opium is a legitimate way of earning a living. Opium farmers in Afghanistan can make approximately twice as much money growing and selling opium as they can for fruit, and make 10 times more than selling wheat. The United Nations Office on Drugs and Crime estimated that in 2006, Afghanistan cultivated more than 400,000 acres of opium, which yielded more than 6,000

(continues)

Figure 2.4.   Afghani opium farmer harvests opium sap in an opium poppy field.   *(© Carol Lee/ Alamy)*

(*continued*)

tons of opium. Following its conversion to heroin, the value of this quantity of heroin was estimated at $3.5 billion (well over half the total income of all of Afghanistan, and approximately 20 percent of this value was given to Afghani opium farmers with the remainder of the proceeds funding the activities of the Taliban). The continued high-volume production of opium in Afghanistan is motivated not only by financial incentives but by national and international political agendas as well. For example, if the Afghani and the multinational forces that currently control Afghanistan were to completely eradicate opium farming, it might produce antigovernment and anti-U.S. sentiment and, without a viable way to support themselves, opium farmers in Afghanistan would likely join forces with the Taliban in their efforts to overthrow the Afghani government and reclaim their rule over Afghanistan.

(*continued from page 25*)
1980s and 1990s, the predominant source of heroin in the United States was Southeast Asia (Burma, Laos, Thailand), and this region accounted for more than 50 percent of the world's opium supply, with an estimated capacity of producing more than 200 metric tons of heroin annually.

PRESCRIPTION OPIATE USE TODAY

In 1970, under the administration of President Richard Nixon, the United States government passed the Controlled Substances Act, which classified all potentially addictive substances into one of five categories, or "schedules" (see Appendix). For example, Schedule I controlled substances are considered to be extremely addictive and to have no accepted medical use, and Schedule II controlled substances are considered to be potentially addictive but do have an accepted medical use. The classification of controlled substances is maintained and constantly updated by the Drug Enforcement Administration (DEA). Currently, heroin is classified as a Schedule I controlled substance. Most other opiate pain relievers, such as morphine, oxycodone, and hydrocodone, are classified as Schedule II controlled substances. There are exceptions, however, such as when codeine is mixed with an over-the-counter pain-relieving drug such as Tylenol (i.e., Co-Tylenol). This mixture is considered a Schedule V controlled substance.

The use of prescription opiates such as morphine, oxycodone, and hydrocodone has steadily increased in recent years, and the nonmedical use of these drugs (that is, for reasons other than pain relief), particularly among high school and college students has caused a great deal of concern among physicians, addiction specialists, and governmental agencies such as the Drug Enforcement Administration. The motives for using opiate pain relievers for nonmedical purposes are generally for relaxation, feeling good or getting high, and experimentation, in addition to relieving pain.[5] The reason for the escalating rates of nonmedical use of opiates in recent years can be attributed to many factors. These include:

1. A lack of education among physicians, pharmacists, and the public at large about the dangers of opiate drugs
2. Physicians overprescribing these medications (for example, a doctor might prescribe an opiate pain reliever when a nonaddictive over-the-counter pain reliever such as Advil or Tylenol might suffice)
3. Ease of obtaining these drugs by drug sharing among young users
4. Stockpiling of opiate medications (that is, taking the drug for only a few days and not disposing of the remaining medication once the pain has subsided).[6]

However, the dangers of nonmedical use of opiate pain relievers are very real. In a report by the Drug Abuse Warning Network (DAWN), more than 300,000 emergency room visits during 2006 were related to the nonmedical use of pain relievers.[7] Efforts by the U.S. government to institute a national prescription monitoring program in an effort to curb overprescription of opiates are currently being made.

SUMMARY

The isolation of morphine as the primary pain relieving component of opium did not occur until early in the eighteenth century, but opium use for pain relief as well as intoxication and nonmedical uses dates back many thousands of years. Ancient writings about and fossils of opium poppies have been found in numerous regions of southwestern Asia and southern Europe, indicating its widespread use. The introduction of opium to China caused power struggles between British-occupied India and China to monopolize the lucrative opium trade, which eventually resulted in the Opium Wars of the eighteenth century. The Chinese are often "blamed" for bringing opium addiction to the United States when they emigrated from China to seek work during the labor shortage caused by the Industrial Revolution. However, it is likely that native people of America may have used opium prior to the arrival of Chinese immigrants. German pharmacist Friedrich Wilhelm Adam Sertürner first isolated morphine as the primary pain relieving component of opium in the early eighteenth century. Morphine was widely used to relieve pain in wounded Civil War soldiers, but its overuse resulted in numerous cases of morphine addiction. In the late 1800s, German pharmaceutical company Bayer synthesized and marketed a chemically modified version of morphine called Heroin as a medicine to treat cough and diarrhea, and the company hoped that Heroin would be less addictive than morphine. This turned out not to be the case, and Heroin addiction soon became a major problem on many continents. The United States first outlawed heroin and limited the dispensing of morphine and other opiate pain relievers to medical doctors with the Harrison Narcotics Act of 1914. The 1970 Controlled Substances Act categorized all illegal and prescription opiates (and other illegal drugs as well, such as cocaine) into one of five schedules, based on the addictive properties of the drug and whether it has any accepted medical value. The illegal trafficking of opium and heroin from numerous countries continues today, and the use of prescription opiate pain relievers such as morphine, oxycodone, and hydrocodone for both legitimate pain-relieving purposes as well as illegal nonmedical use has risen steadily over the past decade.

The Opium Poppy

Oh! just, subtle, and mighty opium! that to the hearts of poor and rich alike, for the wounds that will never heal, and for "the pangs that tempt the spirit to rebel," bringest and assuaging balm; eloquent opium! that with thy potent rhetoric stealest away the purposes of wrath; and to the guilty man, for one night givest back the hopes of his youth, and hands washed pure from blood; and to the proud man, a brief oblivion for wrongs unredress'd, and insults unavenged; that summonest to the chancery of dreams, for the triumphs of suffering innocence, false witnesses; and confoundest perjury; and dost reverse the sentences of unrighteous judges: . . . . Thou only givest these gifts to man; and thou hast the keys of Paradise, oh, just, subtle, and mighty opium!

The preceding passage was taken from a writing by Thomas De Quincey in 1822 called *Confessions of an English Opium Eater*.[1] His enthusiasm for the effects of opium is abundantly clear. This chapter will describe how opium is grown, harvested, and processed into narcotics such as morphine, codeine, and heroin. In addition, a summary of evidence showing that the human body can actually produce the morphine alkaloid chemical will also be given.

GROWING AND HARVESTING OPIUM POPPIES

The scientific name for the opium poppy, *Papaver somniferum*, is derived from the Greek word for poppy, *papaver*, and the Latin term for the ability to produce sleep, *somniferum*.[2] It is an annual plant, meaning that it grows and bears flowers once in its lifetime. Opium poppy seeds are planted densely in large fields at a distance of approximately 8 to 12 inches apart. The plant sprouts from its seeds within two to three weeks of planting. After approximately three months, the plant grows to about two in height and produces flowers with four petals which are usually white, pink, red, or reddish-purple. Only two to four days after the flower blooms, the petals fall to the ground to expose the underlying poppy, which is about the size of a golf ball or chicken egg. It typically takes about four months for the opium poppy to complete its growth cycle, and its final height is usually between two and five feet.

In order to obtain the opium (sometimes called opium **latex**) that is within the poppy, opium farmers must "nick" or incise the plant with a sharp blade (often specialized for this particular purpose and called a *nishtar*), to allow the opium to ooze out. This is typically done around 15 to 21 days after the flower petals have fallen off of the plant. The depth of the cut in the opium poppy must be only about 3 to 4 millimeters. If the cut is too shallow, only a small amount of latex will emerge; if the cut is too deep, the latex will flow into the hollow center of the poppy and cannot be harvested. Often times a single poppy will be incised three to five times to maximize the amount of opium latex that emerges (see Figure 3.1.).

A skilled opium harvester can incise between 150 and 200 opium poppies in an hour. The latex that comes out of the poppy dries into a sticky brown resin, and is usually harvested from one day up to one to two weeks following the cutting of the poppy. This is done by manually scraping the latex off the body of the poppy with a flat piece of metal or wood. Then the latex is collected into a container. Following the harvesting of the opium latex, the plant is left to grow for 20 to 25 days, in order to allow the opium seeds to become fully mature. The opium poppies are then hand-picked, allowed to dry, and threshed to remove and collect the seeds for future opium crops. A single opium poppy can produce upwards of 10,000 opium seeds. Local farmers typically transport the opium to weighing stations where illegal opium traders pay them for their harvest. Or, in some countries where opium production is still legal, the farmers may sell their opium at exchange stations run by the government.

Figure 3.1 Poppy excreting latex. Note how poppy has been cut several times to maximize the amount of opium obtained from each poppy. An opium farmer scrapes the opium latex from an incised opium poppy using a flat piece of metal. *(© Michael S. Yamashita/ Corbis)*

PROCESSING OPIUM LATEX INTO OPIUM AND ITS CHEMICAL COMPONENTS

Approximately 1 to 5 kilograms of raw opium latex is typically harvested from an acre of opium poppies. Raw opium latex contains numerous opiate alkaloids, as shown in Table 3.1.

The concentrations of these chemicals can vary as a result of growing conditions, use of fertilizers, chemical processing methods, and many other factors. Numerous other alkaloids have been found in opium as well, including such chemicals as neopine, codeinone, codamine, salutardine, laudanine, reticuline, palaudine, isoboldine, berberine, and protopine, to name a few.[3] However, each of these chemicals make up less than 0.01 percent of opium.

Table 3.1. Alkaloids Found in Opium and the Approximate Percentage Range of Abundance	
Chemical	Percentage range
Morphine	3.0–25.0
Codeine	0.5–4.0
Narcotine	1.0–12.0
Papaverine	0.5–1.0
Thebaine (Paramorphine)	0.1–2.0
Source: L. D. Kapoor, Opium Poppy: Botany, Chemistry, and Pharmacology (New York: Haworth Press, 1997).	

Opiate pain relievers other than morphine that are frequently prescribed today are derived from one of these five basic chemicals found in opium. For example, oxycodone was first synthesized from thebaine in 1916 and was first used as a pain reliever in 1917. Hydromorphone was first synthesized from morphine in 1921 and was first used as a pain reliever in 1926.[4] And, as discussed in Chapter 2, morphine can also be chemically modified to form the extremely addictive heroin.

As seen in Table 3.1, morphine is the most abundant chemical found in opium. In order to purify it from all the other chemicals, it must be processed and refined in a laboratory. (Many illegal opium dealers can set up such laboratories almost anywhere at relatively little expense.) This process typically involves boiling 10 to 15 kilograms of raw opium in a large barrel or container of water until is dissolves. Chemicals are then added to the liquefied opium that react very specifically with morphine and not with other alkaloids found in opium, which allows the opium processors to isolate the morphine from the chemicals. The solution is then cooled, filtered, heated again, and mixed with additional chemicals, including hydrochloric acid. Morphine then forms solid matter in the solution known as morphine hydrochloride. This is usually pressed into bricks, wrapped in cloth or paper, and most often further processed into heroin by a relatively simple and quick procedure using easily available industrial chemicals.

POPPY SEEDS

Although most people are generally unaware of it, the poppy seeds that are commonly found on bagels, muffins, breads, and cakes are actually seeds from the opium poppy. After the cultivation of the opium latex, opium poppies are usually harvested for their seeds. A single opium poppy can produce more than 10,000 poppy seeds, and many cultures use the tremendous amount of seeds produced by the opium harvest for cooking and baking.

A typical poppy seed roll contains approximately three-quarters of a gram of poppy seeds. Although poppy seeds do contain trace amounts of opiate alkaloids, there is not nearly enough opiate in this

(continues)

Figure 3.2. Poppy seeds found in many baked goods such as bagels and muffins come from the opium poppy, but do not contain nearly enough opiate alkaloids to produce pain-relieving or other effects of prescription strength morphine. *(© Juanmonino/ stockphoto)*

(continued)

amount of poppy seed to produce pain relief or euphoria. However, eating foods that contain poppy seeds can cause people to fail a drug test. Experiments conducted on the television shows *MythBusters* and *Brainiac: Science Abuse* showed that people can indeed test positive for opiates after eating two to four poppy seed bagels or rolls. Although food processing reduces the content of opiate alkaloids such as morphine by more than 90 percent, advances in scientific technologies have allowed for the detection of opiate alkaloids in urine samples as low as a billionth of a gram. This can produce false positives in people who do not take opiate drugs, resulting in problems with employment or athletic event screening procedures. In addition, opiate addicts who are attempting to stay abstinent from using these drugs can test positive for opiates after eating enough poppy seed foods, even if they have stopped taking the opiate drug. This can lead to problems for people who are required to have opiate-negative drug screens for legal reasons, such as parolees from jail or participants in drug addiction treatment programs.[5] Scientists are currently exploring ways to differentiate positive urine screens from people who are actually using opiate drugs versus those who might have had a few poppy seed rolls the day before a drug test.

ENDOGENOUS OPIATE ALKALOIDS: DOES THE BODY PRODUCE ITS OWN MORPHINE?

A chemical or substance is described as **endogenous** when it is naturally produced by one or more organs, tissues, or fluids in the body. This is in contrast to the term **exogenous**, which means that the chemical or substance, if found within a tissue, fluid, or organ in the body, cannot be manufactured by the body and must be obtained from the environment. Since the 1970s, scientists have found that vertebrate creatures (cats, rats, mice, humans), as well as invertebrates such as mussels, produce trace amounts of opiate alkaloids, including morphine and other chemicals found in opium, among them thebaine, codeine, reticuline, and salutardine.[6] Such chemicals have been found in minute quantities in tissues of the nervous and immune systems. Although various opiate alkaloids have been found, they are generally termed **endogenous morphine**. As with the opiate alkaloids, the concentrations of endogenous morphine in the body are so low that they are unlikely to produce any kind of pain-relieving effects, sedation, or euphoria. Yet scientists are puzzled by the fact that these chemicals are synthesized even by the numerous species that do not inject heroin, take opiate pain relievers, or eat poppy seed foods. To date, most scientists believe that endogenous morphine plays the role of a neurotransmitter or a hormone in the nervous and immune systems.[7] However, the precise function of endogenous morphine still remains a mystery.

SUMMARY

The opium poppy is an annual plant that flowers and then bears a poppy that is rich in opium. Opium poppy plants are grown on many continents and harvested for the saplike latex substance, which contains many opiate alkaloids, the most abundant of which is morphine. Chemical processing is used to purify the morphine from the opium latex and, most often, further transform it into the illegal and highly addictive drug heroin. Trace amounts of opiate alkaloids, including morphine, are found in poppy seeds, which are frequently used in baked goods such as bagels, muffins, breads, and cakes. Finally, morphine and other opiate alkaloids have been found to be produced in minute amounts in the tissues of several invertebrate and vertebrate animals, including humans.

4
Biological Effects of Morphine

Katie was a 28-year-old single female who worked as a registered nurse at the county hospital in Boulder, Colorado. One of her favorite recreational activities was snowboarding, and one weekend while snowboarding at a local resort she had a bad fall and sprained some muscles in her lower back. Her injuries were not life-threatening, but members of the ski patrol had to take her on a sled down to the medical station at the base of the ski resort. She was prescribed morphine for the pain in her back. Katie missed several days of work because the morphine was so sedating, but without it her back caused her so much pain she was unable sit or stand. The following week, she felt like she could return to work and use the morphine to cope with her back pain. The morphine allowed her to sit for several hours at a time, but it made her feel nauseous at times and her skin often felt itchy. She also found that the drug made her feel groggy and unable to think clearly, so much that she could only perform desk duties instead of attending to patients. After about one week back at work while still taking morphine, one day she felt like trying to go to work without taking her morphine so as to avoid the side effects, and instead took an over-the-counter pain reliever. However, that day at work, her back pain returned, she felt extremely miserable, was easily irritated, and had frequent diarrhea. Katie was beginning to show signs of dependence on morphine.

Morphine's pain-relieving and pleasurable effects are due to its actions on the nervous system, but morphine also has biological effects in many other systems of the body. Before discussing the biological effects of morphine on the nervous system, a basic overview of how nerve cells communicate is given. Effects of morphine on the rest of the body will then be discussed.

HOW NERVE CELLS IN THE BRAIN WORK

In the brain, **neurons** carry electrical signals along wirelike nerve fibers called **axons**. Axons can range from less than a millimeter in length to several centimeters. At the end of each axon is a mushroom-shaped nerve ending called a **synaptic** or **axon terminal**. When the electrical signal traveling down the axon reaches the synaptic terminal, it causes chemical messengers, called **neurotransmitters**, which are normally stored in sphere-like packages called **vesicles**, to be released and secreted onto nearby neurons. This junction between a synaptic terminal and a nearby neuron is called a **synapse**.

There are billions of synapses in the brain, and each neuron can have as many as 10,000 different synapses on it. After neurotransmitters are released, they diffuse away from the synaptic terminal into the synapse and encounter proteins called **receptors** on the surface of nearby neurons. Receptors are specific proteins that are designed to recognize specific neurotransmitters. Receptors are usually located on **dendrites**, which are branched fibers designed to receive numerous signals from other neurons, or on the **cell body** of the neuron, which contains various cell components including genetic material (chromosomes composed of DNA) that is found in the **nucleus** (see Figure 4.1.). When activated by neurotransmitters, these receptors can cause the nerve cell on which they reside to either become activated (so it passes along the electrical signal) or inhibited (so it does not pass the signal along).

THE BRAIN AND ITS OWN OPIATE SYSTEMS

Morphine binds to and activates a receptor called the **mu (μ) opioid** or **opiate receptor**. This receptor is normally the receptor protein that binds endogenous neurotransmitters such as endorphins and enkephalins. It is well known that highly stressful events, intense physical exercise, and even taking addictive drugs can cause the release of endorphins and enkephalins in the brain, which can have pain-relieving and pleasurable effects (such as the "runner's high" experienced by long-distance or avid joggers). By directly activating mu opiate receptors, morphine mimics the actions of endorphins and enkephalins. The brain and spinal cord, which together make up the **central nervous system (CNS)**, contain high amounts of mu opiate receptors that are distributed

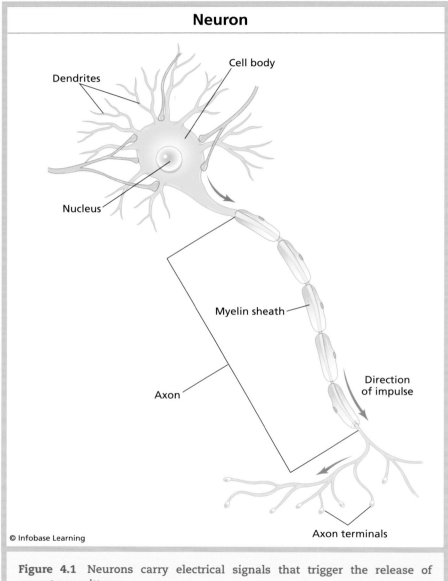

Neuron

© Infobase Learning

Figure 4.1 Neurons carry electrical signals that trigger the release of neurotransmitters.

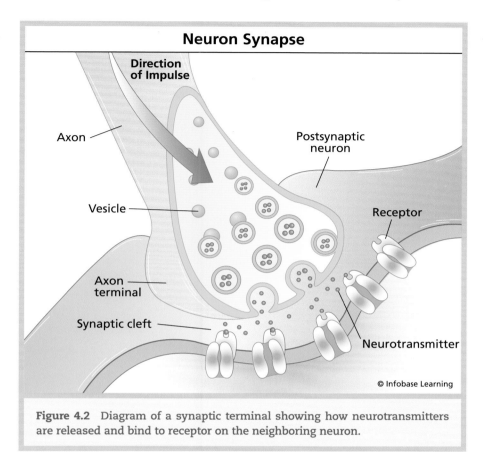

Figure 4.2 Diagram of a synaptic terminal showing how neurotransmitters are released and bind to receptor on the neighboring neuron.

widely across the various regions of the brain (see Table 4.1 for a list of the major regions of the brain and their function, as depicted in Figure 4.3).

PSYCHOLOGICAL EFFECTS

One of the most important effects of morphine is its ability to reduce or eliminate the perception of the sense of pain. This will be discussed in great detail in Chapter 5. Morphine can also cause intense feelings of well-being and euphoria, which often leads to the desire to keep using morphine, which ultimately results in addiction to morphine (discussed more in Chapter 6). However, morphine produces a number of other psychological effects, many

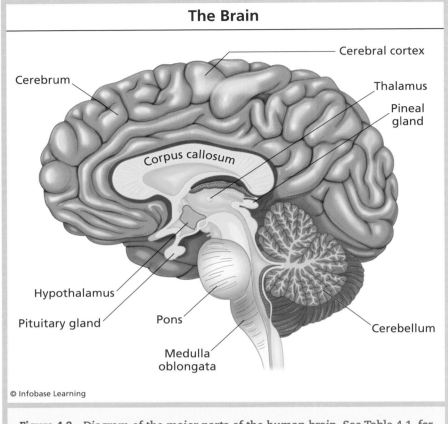

The Brain

Cerebral cortex

Cerebrum

Thalamus

Pineal gland

Corpus callosum

Hypothalamus

Pituitary gland

Pons

Medulla oblongata

Cerebellum

© Infobase Learning

Figure 4.3   Diagram of the major parts of the human brain. See Table 4.1. for a description of the functions of the major regions of the brain.

of which can be considered unwanted **side effects**.[1] The first of these are **sedation** and **drowsiness**, since morphine has a general depressant effect on the activity of the nervous system. Although the sedative effects of morphine can dissipate with repeated taking of the same dose of the drug (known as tolerance; see Chapter 5), the sedative effects often result in impaired quality of life and a desire to stop taking the medication. Ironically, although morphine is sedating, it actually causes **sleep disturbances** because it reduces the amount of time the user spends in certain stages of sleep, particularly rapid eye movement (REM) sleep, which is when dreams occur. The sedating and sleep-altering effects of morphine are believed to take place in the

Table 4.1 Main Regions of the Brain and their Function	
Region	Function
cerebrum	largest part of the brain, consisting of a left and right hemisphere
cerebral cortex	outermost wrinkled part of the brain where planning, thinking, and information processes occur
corpus callosum	bundle of nerve fibers that connects the left and right hemispheres of the cerebrum
pineal gland	controls biological rhythms such as sleeping and waking, secretes the hormone melatonin
cerebellum	controls motor coordination and balance
medulla oblongata, pons, and midbrain	control basic bodily functions like chewing, swallowing, heart rate, motivation, and breathing; collectively known as the brain stem
pituitary gland	secretes hormones that control many bodily functions such as growth, metabolism, and reproduction
hypothalamus	controls metabolism, sleeping, hunger, thirst, and body temperature
thalamus	acts as a relay station for all incoming information from the senses (touch, vision, hearing, etc.)

brain stem, which controls sleep and levels of arousal. The sedating effects of morphine also result in impaired **psychomotor performance**, such as the ability to drive a car or perform tasks that require concentration and coordination.

There is some controversy over whether morphine, if taken in high doses or on a long-term basis, actually causes damage to the brain. Brain damage as a result of chronic use of other drugs such as cocaine, methamphetamine, Ecstasy, and alcohol is much more clear than the damage caused by morphine. Numerous studies conducted in laboratory animals and cells grown in petri dishes have shown that high doses of morphine can indeed cause nerve cells to die.[2] However, some scientists question whether the concentrations and doses of morphine used in these studies are equivalent to those that human morphine users are exposed to. While some researchers have reported evidence of disturbed nerve cell function and alterations in the physical structure of the brain in heroin addicts, evidence for long-lasting damage or **toxicity** in the brain of morphine addicts has not yet been clearly and repeatedly demonstrated.[3] However, a few studies have indicated that long-term opiate use can produce some evidence of diminished mental function. For example, two studies conducted in Denmark showed that patients receiving daily doses of an average of 60 milligrams of morphine (or equivalent amounts of other opiate pain relievers) showed reduced performance on standard laboratory tests of attention, memory, and reaction times.[4]

PHYSIOLOGICAL EFFECTS

Opiates have numerous actions outside the central nervous system (the brain and spinal cord), and these can also be classified as unwanted side effects.[5] Mu opiate receptors are also expressed in many regions of the **peripheral nervous system**, which is the division of the nervous system that is outside the skull and spinal cord and is made up nerves that transmit information to the brain from the skin, muscles, and internal organs, as well as send information out to these parts of the body. Some of our internal organs contain high levels of mu opiate receptors, including the intestines. By activating mu opiate receptors in the intestines, morphine causes the passage of digested food through the intestines to slow down. The intestines reabsorb some of the water contained in the digested food, which produces **constipation**, or difficulty in excreting solid waste from the body. Constipation is a significant problem for many people who take morphine or other opiate pain relievers, particularly on a long-term basis, since it can cause complications such as formation of **hemorrhoids** (painful, swollen veins in the lower portion of the rectum or anus), or intestinal bleeding or rupture, which can lead to death. The constipation caused by morphine and other opiates is most often treated with laxatives. Another frequent problem in the digestive system that is caused by morphine is **nausea**, a sensation of unease and discomfort in the stomach accompanied an urge to vomit. Some people actually experience vomiting (also known as **emesis**) as a result of taking opiate drugs.

Morphine and other opiates cause **respiratory depression** (decreased breathing rates and shallow breaths) by inhibiting the activity of nerve cells in the brain stem that control breathing. This can result in accumulation of fluid in the lungs and increase the chance of developing infections of the respiratory system such as **pneumonia**. Most deaths caused by an overdose of opiate drugs, including morphine, are a result of a complete stoppage of respiration caused by the drug shutting down the ability of the brain stem to control breathing. Similarly, opiates such as morphine inhibit the cough reflex, which is also controlled by the brain stem, and for this reason opiates are sometimes given as cough suppressants (also known as **antitussive** agents).

Other physiological effects of opiates are **bladder dysfunctions** such as **urinary retention** (reduced ability to urinate). As with respiratory depression, urinary retention is believed to be a result of opiates inhibiting the areas of the brain stem that control bladder function.[6] Morphine can also cause cells of the immune systems to release a chemical called **histamine**, which causes uncomfortable itching sensations (called **pruritus**) in the skin. In addition, chronic use of morphine can cause **immunosuppresion** (reduced activity of the immune system), which compromises the ability of the body to fight off infections caused by bacteria or viruses. Opiates also cause the pupils to shrink to pinpoint size, known as **pupillary constriction** (sometimes called **miosis**, not to be confused with "meiosis," which refers to a process of how cells form duplicates of themselves).[7] Finally, opiates can reduce blood pressure below normal levels, a condition known as **hypotension**.

METABOLISM OF MORPHINE

Morphine is metabolized by the liver into two primary metabolites, morphine-3-glucuronide (**M3G**) and morphine-6-glucuronide (**M6G**).[8] The metabolites are formed with the help of a liver enzyme called uridine 5'-diphospho-glucuronosyltransferase (sometimes shortened to UDP-glucuronosyltransferase or UGT). M3G is inactive and has no biological effects, but is produced in higher quantities than M6G. M6G, on the other hand, is a potent activator of the mu opiate receptor, which may contribute to and prolong the effects of morphine. M6G has been shown to have many effects similar to that of morphine, including pain relief and respiratory depression.[9] Thus, M6G is considered an **active metabolite** of morphine. Both M6G and M3G are eliminated from the body in the urine.

DRUG HALF-LIVES

Drugs are often referred to as "short-acting" or "long-lasting" based on their **half-life**, which is the amount of time it takes for the body to metabolize and/or excrete half the amount of the substance that has been ingested. Short-acting opiates include morphine, hydromorphone, oxycodone, fentanyl, codeine, and meperidine; long-acting opiates include methadone, propoxyphene, and levorphanol. The half-life of morphine is approximately two to three hours, which means if a person took morphine and achieved a peak blood concentration of morphine of 1 milligram per deciliter (mg/dl), it would take two to three hours for that concentration of morphine to be broken down and reduced to 0.5 mg/dl. However, it does not take just two half-lives for the body to rid itself of a substance entirely. After an additional two to three hours, the concentration of morphine would be 0.25 mg/dl, then in another two to three hours it would be 0.125 mg/dl, and so on. Therefore, it can take many half-lives for the body to metabolize or excrete a drug to a point where it is no longer detectable in the blood. Different opiate pain relievers have different half-lives. The half-lives of oxycodone and hydrocodone are three to four and a half hours, slightly longer than that of morphine. On the other hand, the half-life of methadone, which is often used to treat opiate addiction, is 24–36 hours, making it extremely long-lasting. The morphine metabolite M6G has a half-life of about four hours, and since M6G is an active metabolite that activates the mu opiate receptor, it can prolong the effects of morphine. In addition to influencing how long the psychological and physiological effects of a drug will last, the half-life of a drug also determines how long it can be detected in the blood. This is important information in the event that the drug user must undergo a drug test for employment, eligibility for participation in sports, and the like.

Source: C. E. Inturrisi, "Clinical Pharmacology of Opioids for Pain," *Clinical Journal of Pain* 18, 4 Suppl (2002): S3–13.

SUMMARY

Morphine binds to and activates the mu opiate receptor, which is a protein that is normally activated by the brain's endogenous opiate-like neurotransmitters such as endorphins and enkephalins. Morphine can produce euphoria and potent relief from pain, but also has numerous unwanted psychological side effects such as sedation, drowsiness, sleep disturbances, and impaired psychomotor performance. In addition, morphine has many unwanted physiological side effects such as constipation, nausea, respiratory depression, bladder dysfunction, itching, and suppression of the functioning of the immune system. Morphine is metabolized by the liver into M3G and M6G, the latter of which is an active metabolite that also binds to the mu opiate receptor.

5
Morphine as an Analgesic

John was a computer programmer who severely sprained his knee while skateboarding, and his doctor prescribed him morphine which he took daily. John soon began to experience tolerance to the pain-relieving effects of morphine. His doctor originally prescribed him pills containing 10 milligrams of morphine to be taken three times a day. However, by the end of the first week of taking morphine, its ability to relieve his knee pain began to diminish, and he became increasingly uncomfortable with amount of pain he was experiencing. He reported this to his doctor, who increased his dose to 15 milligrams of morphine to be taken three times a day. With this increased dose, the pain in John's knee was dramatically reduced, but he also felt increasingly groggy and experienced constipation. His doctor recommended drinking prune juice as a natural laxative, which seemed to help. However, because John's finances were tight, he needed to work and could not afford to take more time off. So he continued to work, even though the doctor recommended he let the sprained muscles in his knee heal by staying at home and resting on his bed. So John continued taking morphine and within another week he noticed his knee pain returning, and when she complained to his doctor about this, he reluctantly increased John's dose to 20 milligrams, fearing that the tolerance to the effects of morphine he was experiencing and the unexpected length of time he required the morphine for pain relief might cause him to become addicted to the morphine.

Pain comes in many forms, such as a shooting pain when we step barefooted on a nail or accidentally bite our tongue. Or it comes on as a dull and uncomfortable ache after a muscle injury. The English language contains many words to describe pain. Pain can be described as nagging, sharp, burning, aching, gnawing, stinging, throbbing, pounding, shooting, stabbing, excruciating, and agonizing, among many other terms. Despite being a very unpleasant sensation, pain is very helpful and adaptive response. Human beings as a species would likely not have survived for very long without the sensation of pain. Pain tells us when something is injuring or damaging our skin, muscle, and other tissues and organs. For example, pain keeps us from burning our hands when lighting a match or starting a fire. Tooth pain tells us we might have a cavity or more serious problem with our teeth. Stomach pain tells us we may have eaten something poisonous or that we may have an ulcer. Chest pain tells us we might be having a heart attack. Due to their unpleasant nature, pain signals are good at getting our attention, and we immediately look for ways to get rid of them. It is because of pain we avoid hurting ourselves, damaging our tissues and organs, and become aware of possible disorders or diseases that might be occurring in our bodies.

Despite being a very helpful sensation, most of us develop a natural fear of pain, and we subsequently shape much of our behavior around avoiding pain. We often avoid places, situations, or objects that are associated with previously painful experiences. For example, we avoid going to the dentist so we don't have to experience dental pain, which often is very uncomfortable. Or, we avoid going to see a doctor for an allergy shot or immunization because we fear the pain of needles in our skin or muscles.

Although pain is rooted in biology, it is not a sensation that every individual experiences the same way. The perception of pain to different types of injury or tissue damage varies widely from person to person. Cultural and psychological factors play a large role in how we experience pain (or at least how we show it). Many cultures, both ancient and modern, have ceremonies and rituals in which individuals (usually adolescent boys or young men) must endure extreme pain and physical demands, without emitting so much as a whimper, in order to become an "adult," "man," or "soldier." In sports and athletics, pain is seen as something that strengthens our character, talents, and abilities—hence the common slogan "No pain, no gain." Ironically, while enduring large amounts of pain has traditionally been viewed as characteristic of being a "man," it is the female gender that has to endure one of the most painful experiences possible—childbirth.

Before discussing how morphine and other opiates act as pain relievers, we will first discuss types of severe and **chronic pain** that often require opiate analgesics such as morphine rather than milder over-the-counter remedies such as aspirin.

TYPES OF CHRONIC PAIN

Numerous times in our lives, we all experience **acute pain** that is short-lived—such as pain from a scratch, a paper cut, a hangnail, falling off a bike, getting hit with a baseball, a sprained ankle, or menstrual cramps. Acute pain lasts from a few seconds to a few hours, days, or sometimes a week or two. Some types of acute pain can be recurrent, such as a migraine headache, occurring for relatively short periods of time but returning at frequent intervals.

Fortunately, acute pain goes away relatively quickly, either on its own or with the help of medications or other treatments, and we can soon resume normal daily functioning. However, millions of people suffer from some form of chronic pain that lasts for weeks, months, or years. Chronic pain causes not only terrible suffering to the individual, but severe economic and social consequences, such as lost productivity at work and high costs of medical treatment. Chronic pain often results in depression, addiction to pain medications, and, in rare instances, suicide. Chronic pain is usually divided into two classifications: malignant and nonmalignant. **Malignant chronic pain** refers to pain that is a result of cancer, while **nonmalignant chronic pain** is a general term that refers to chronic pain that is a result of medical conditions other than cancer. Below are some medical conditions that are characterized by chronic pain and are often treated with opiates.

Cancer

Cancer cells are very much like normal cells in the body, except they multiply out of control, causing the formation of tumors. These tumors eventually grow large enough to put pressure on nerve endings, blood vessels, air passages in the lungs, and the sensitive covering of bones, causing pain. Cancer can also damage nerve fibers themselves, and this nerve damage (called **neuropathy**) causes pain. Cancer cells can also invade the body's normal tissues and destroy internal organs, which can also cause significant chronic pain.

Amputation

Occasionally, amputation of a limb (arm or leg) becomes medically necessary following a traumatic accident or injury, to stop the spread of cancer, or because of severe disease in the limb's tissue or blood vessels. The process of surgically removing the limb severs major nerve fibers. Initially, amputation results in sensations known as **phantom limb syndrome**, where the patient still feels (usually quite convincingly) that the limb is still attached. At first, this phantom limb phenomenon is not painful but is very confusing to the patient. Over time, the nerve fibers that once supplied the now missing limb attempt to grow back into the limb, but these nerves ultimately grow into various tangles and result in the formation of tender spots on the limb stump. These newly sprouted nerve fibers can spontaneously and mistakenly send pain signals to the brain in the form of violent stabs or constant burning or cramping.

Headaches

Although all people get some type of headache once in a while, some people experience headaches that are so severe they can hinder a person's ability to think or function. The most common type of severe headache is **migraine**. Migraines afflict millions of people and occur more commonly in women. Migraines tend to run in families as well. The precise causes of migraine headaches are unknown, but are suspected to be a result of inflammation or sudden dilation of the blood vessels surrounding the brain. Migraines have many known triggers, such as bright lights, certain foods, changes in weather or climate, alcohol, hormonal changes, hunger, stress, and lack of sleep. Most migraine sufferers describe their headaches as a throbbing or pulsating pain that starts in a specific area of the head which later spreads over the rest of the head. Migraines tend to intensify over a one- to two-hour period (sometimes longer), and then gradually subside. People with migraines often feel nauseous and highly sensitive to light, sounds, or odors. After the migraine passes, the sufferer is left feeling weak and drained. A migraine can incapacitate a person for an entire day. A subset of migraine sufferers experience an "aura" (bright shimmering lights in their peripheral vision, wavy or zigzag lines, hallucinations, or muscle weakness or numbness) about 10 to 30 minutes before the onset of the migraine. It is unknown how this aura relates to the cause or symptoms of a migraine.

Backaches

As with headaches, pain in the back (especially the lower back) occurs in almost everyone at some point in their life, whether from overstraining oneself while lifting a heavy object, injuring oneself while participating in sports, sleeping on an uncomfortable surface, and so on. However, some back pain is chronic and takes weeks, months, or even years to recover from. Back pain is usually caused by a compressed nerve, slipped vertebral disc, fracture of a vertebra, muscle strain, infection, tumor, or arthritis. Chronic back pain can be very severe and result in the inability to sit, stand, or lie down comfortably, and often alters one's posture.

Arthritis

Arthritis is a general term used to describe chronic pain in the joints such as the fingers, wrists, elbows, shoulders, knees, ankles, or feet. There are two type of arthritis—**rheumatoid arthritis**, which results from an inflammation of the thin membranes lining the joints, and **osteoarthritis**, which is the more common type of arthritis resulting from a progressive breakdown of the cushions of cartilage between bones in particular joints. Both types of arthritis can be extremely painful and result in stiffness, limited motion, and fatigue.

Fibromyalgia

Fibromyalgia (pronounced fy-bro-my-al-jee-ah) is a medical condition that causes aching or burning pain in many parts of the body, such as the neck, shoulders, chest, back, hips, hands and feet. Millions of people suffer from fibromyalgia, and most of the sufferers are women between the ages of 20 and 40. Fibromyalgia patients have poor sleep patterns because of their constant pain, and are therefore fatigued and sleepy during the day. The pain from fibromyalgia is often worse in the morning, better during the day, then worse again at night. The cause of fibromyalgia is unknown but may involve malfunctions of the immune system or spinal cord.

Trigeminal neuralgia

Trigeminal neuralgia is a medical condition that results in terrible pain in the face, particularly a stabbing sensation on one side of the face that feels almost like an electric shock. These painful episodes begin and end rather quickly, but they are recurrent. Once suspected to be a result of malfunctioning of the major nerve that has many nerve endings in the face (the trigeminal nerve), most evidence to date suggest that the cause of trigeminal neuralgia is a compression or deterioration of the trigeminal nerve.

Shingles

Shingles is a painful condition caused by the chicken pox virus. People who were exposed to the chicken pox virus as children often have small amounts of dormant (inactive) virus particles around their spinal cord, even as adults. For reasons still not clear, stress, cancer, or infection with the human immunodeficiency virus (HIV) causes these chicken pox viruses to become active, multiply, and migrate along nerve fibers extending from the spinal cord to the skin. Here, the virus produces a temporary band of redness and inflammation, which subsequently dies down and forms scar tissue. However, during this process, some of the nerve endings in the skin become damaged and result in chronic pain.

PAIN TERMINOLOGY

The medical term for the perception of pain is **nociception**, or the perception of **noxious** (unpleasant, painful) sensations. Thus, the nerve endings in the skin, muscle, and internal organs that respond to painful stimuli are called **nociceptors**. A state of reduced or eliminated perception of pain without the loss of consciousness is called **analgesia**, and thus pain relievers are often called analgesics. Analgesia is different from **anesthesia**, which eliminates pain sensations as well as all other sensations (touch, pressure, temperature, and so on), causing numbness if a local anesthetic is used, or loss of consciousness if a general anesthetic used, such as during a major surgical procedure. However, the terms analgesia and anesthesia are often mistakenly used interchangeably. Finally, the term **hyperalgesia** is used to describe a state in which a normally nonpainful sensation, such as gently touching one's skin or moving a joint, becomes very painful because of inflammation or tissue damage. Examples of hyperalgesia are sunburned skin or a sprained ankle.

THE ANATOMY OF PAIN

Pain signals originate in nociceptors located on nerve endings in the skin, muscles, the thin coating of bones, and in internal organs. When activated by tissue damage, burns, mechanical disruption, or extreme pressure or temperatures, nociceptors send signals along the long sensory nerve fibers to the spinal cord. The sensory nerve fibers that transmit pain signals can be divided into two types: **A-delta (A-δ) fibers**, which are insulated with the fatty substance myelin and transmit fast pain signals (2 to 30 meters per second) to give the sensation of sharp, localized pain; and **C-fibers**, which are not insulated with myelin and conduct pain signals at a slower speed (0.5 to 2 meters per second) to produce the sensation of slower, burning pain. Some sensory nerve fibers (such as those extending from the spinal cord to the toes) are more than a meter long, whereas others (such as those from the teeth to the brain stem) are only a few inches long. Sensory nerve fibers enter the spinal cord and connect to the **dorsal horn**. Here, the nerve fibers make synapses onto neurons called **interneurons**, which then relay the information to other neurons that transmit the pain signal up to the brain. Nerve fibers carrying pain signals enter the via the brain and make connection in a region of the brain called the **thalamus**, which is essentially a "relay station" for all sensory information coming into the brain. From there, signals are transmitted on to the **cerebral cortex**, where the information is perceived and processed on a conscious level, allowing the person to experience and react to the pain.

MORPHINE AND OTHER OPIATES AS PAIN RELIEVERS

Doctors are most likely to prescribe morphine or other opiates when pain is severe and expected to be short (lasting a few days to a week), such as after an injury or major surgery. This is because short-term use of opiates is less likely to lead to tolerance (loss of the ability to relieve pain following repeated taking of the same dose of the drug) and **dependence** (addiction). However, the use of opiates as pain relievers becomes more problematic in cases of chronic pain, since long-term use of opiates most often results in tolerance to the pain-relieving effects as well as physical dependence and addiction.

Mu opiate receptors are located on the surface of nerve cells in the dorsal horn of the spinal cord, where sensory nerve fibers from the skin, muscle, internal organs, and the like enter the spinal cord before sending their signals to the brain. Activation of the mu opiate receptor by opiate drugs such as morphine reduces the activity of the nerve cells that they are located on (the

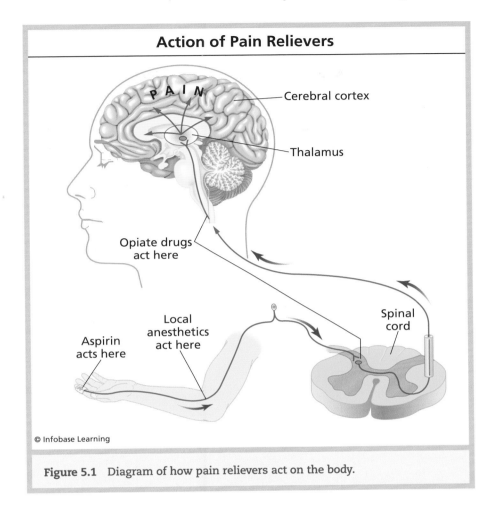

Action of Pain Relievers

© Infobase Learning

Figure 5.1 Diagram of how pain relievers act on the body.

pain fibers entering the dorsal horn of the spinal cord), and thus the transmission of pain signals to the brain is greatly reduced or eliminated. Mu opiate receptors are also located on neurons in various regions of the brain that process pain signals, including the thalamus and cerebral cortex, and therefore opiates can reduce the perception of pain by acting in the brain as well as in the dorsal horn of the spinal cord.

Table 5.1 gives a list of commonly used opiate pain relievers, including morphine, along with their brand names, typical dosages, and duration of analgesia.[1] These drugs are mostly given in the form of a pill, tablet, or

Table 5.1 Opiate Pain Relievers

Drug name	Common brand name(s)	Typical oral dose range (mg)	Duration of analgesia (hours)	Comments
buprenorphine	Buprenex, Suboxone	4–32 mg	6–40	25–40 times more potent than morphine; Suboxone recently approved for treatment of opiate addiction; can also be given as long-lasting skin patch
codeine	none	8–64	4–6	2–3 times less potent than morphine; often combined with acetaminophen (Co-Tylenol); has active metabolites including morphine
fentanyl	Sublimaze, Duragesic	0.01–0.1	48–72 (as skin patch) 1–2 (regular form)	80 times more potent than morphine; also sold in western Europe in a lollipop form under the brand name Actiq; other formulations such as an aerosol spray and an under-the-tongue patch have been developed
hydrocodone	Vicodin	5–10	3–6	roughly the same potency as morphine; one of the most commonly used opiates for pain relief
hydromorphone	Dilaudid, Palladone	2–10	3–6 12–24 (ER* form)	7–10 times more potent than morphine; high doses can cause seizures and muscle spasms
levorphanol	Levo-Dromoran	2–4	4–15	4–8 times more potent than morphine
meperidine	Demerol	50–100	3–6	10 times less potent than morphine; produces toxic metabolites, cannot be used with older types of antidepressants such as monoamine oxidase inhibitors

methadone	Dolophine, Amidone, Methadose	80–120	4–8	has slightly less potency than morphine, can penetrate into fatty tissues and thus have a very long half-life (12–150 hours), very often used for treatment of opiate addiction
morphine	Roxane	10–60	3–6 (regular form)	active metabolite is M6G
oxycodone	Oxycontin	5–30	3–6 (regular form) 8–12 (ER form)	potency roughly equivalent to that of morphine; often combined with aspirin (Percodan) or acetaminophen (Percocet), has three times better absorption from stomach into bloodstream than morphine
oxymorphone	Numorphan, Opana	1–40	4–6 (regular form) 12–36 (ER form)	5–10 times more potent than morphine, is an active metabolite of oxycodone
propoxyphene	Darvon	30–100	4–6	5–10 times less potent than morphine; often combined with acetaminophen (Darvocet), long-acting metabolite norpropoxyphene can be toxic to heart
tramadol	Ultram	100–400	4–6 (regular form) 24 (ER form)	5–10 times less potent than morphine, active metabolite O-demethyl tramadol is primarily responsible for analgesic effects

* ER = extended release formulation

Source: T. H. Stanley, "Fentanyl," Journal of Pain and Symptom Management 29, 5 Suppl. (2005): S67–71; E. Kalso, "Oxycodone," Journal of Pain and Symptom Management 29, 5 Suppl. (2005): S47–56; A. Murray and N. A. Hagen, "Hydromorphone," Journal of Pain and Symptom Management 29, 5 Suppl (2005): S57–66.

capsule, but can also be injected intravenously or directly into the spinal fluid (discussed below). These opiate pain relievers differ primarily in their duration of action and the dosage required to obtain sufficient pain relief.

CONTROLLING YOUR OWN LEVEL OF PAIN

Normally, opiate pain relievers are given to nonhospitalized patients in the form of a pill or tablet, which can take 30 to 60 minutes to start working. If the patient is in the hospital, opiates are usually given intravenously by a doctor or nurse. In this case, when the pain-relieving effects of the opiate wear off, the doctor or nurse must be summoned to give the patient another dose. However, technological advances since the 1990s have allowed doctors and scientists to develop a method for allowing the patient to control the intravenous administration of the pain medication. This technique is called **patient-controlled analgesia (PCA)**.[3] In PCA, the pain medication (typically morphine, fentanyl, or fentanyl derivatives) is dissolved into a solution and put in a syringe that is located in a computerized syringe pump. The syringe is connected to plastic tubing and a hypodermic needle or catheter that has been placed into a vein (usually in the patient's wrist or forearm; see Figure 5.2). When the patient pushes a button on a remote control device, the syringe pump automatically delivers a specific amount of the drug solution into the patient's bloodstream. In this way, whenever the patient begins to feel pain, more pain medication is only the click of a button away.

However, PCA does not allow the patient to administer as much of the drug as he or she would like. To avoid overdosing, the doctor specifies how much drug is delivered with each dose, and the syringe pump has a "lockout" mechanism that keeps the syringe from delivering any more drug for a specific amount of time (usually for 5 to 10 minutes).

The advantages of PCA are that the patient is able to voluntarily control the precise amount of pain medication needed to control his or her pain without having to summon the doctor or nurse every time an injection is needed. This allows for maintaining more constant levels of pain medication in the bloodstream. Also, since the pain relieving and side effects of various opiates can vary widely from one patient to another, PCA allows the patient to inject more or less of the

Some of the shorter-acting opiates have specially modified into an extended release (ER) as controlled release formulations, which prolongs their duration of pain-relieving effects.

drug as dictated by his or her individual needs. Finally, many patients, particularly those with cancer, find that having control over their own pain relief gives them greater peace of mind and a sense of control over their own suffering. The method of PCA has been extended to the use of sedatives (called patient-controlled sedation, or PCS) for people who are anticipating undergoing an unpleasant surgical medical procedure such as dental surgery or colonoscopy.[4]

In recent years, advances in manipulating the chemical properties of opiates have enabled doctors to "volatilize," or make an opiate drug airborne, so it can be delivered as an aerosol spray into the nose. This method of delivery is more desirable than intravenous PCA since it does not require expensive equipment or intravenous catheters. Successes have been reported using aerosolized fentanyl and oxycodone nasal sprays as alternative methods for PCA.[5]

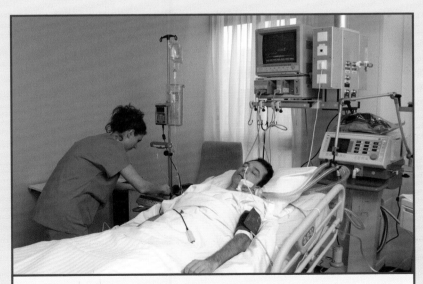

Figure 5.2 Patient-controlled analgesia allows the patient more control over pain relief. *(© LADA/ Hop Americain/ Photo Researchers, Inc.)*

Due to the known toxic metabolites produced by the breakdown of meperidine and propoxyphene, these opiates are rarely prescribed today. For people with health insurance, the average cost of filling a prescription for an opiate is approximately $10, but for those without insurance, the costs can range from $12 to $60, depending on the medication.[2] Patients who are prescribed extended-release formulations of opiates pay about double these amounts due to the fact that generic (non-brand-name) forms of these medications are not yet available, and that these medications are more costly to manufacture.

If a particular patient develops tolerance to the pain-relieving effects of a particular opiate, many doctors will "rotate" the patient between different drugs: They may prescribe morphine for one week, oxycodone for the next, hydrocodone for the third, and so on, in an effort to minimize the tolerance. This is known as **opiate rotation**. However, this strategy does not work for all patients with chronic pain, since some people develop what is known as **cross-tolerance**, or the development of tolerance to the effects of other drugs similar to the opiate being currently used even though that particular opiate drug may not have been previously taken. Cross-tolerance occurs between different opiate pain relievers because most of these drugs have similar chemical structures and act on the same biological target (the mu opiate receptor).

EPIDURAL ADMINISTRATION OF OPIATES

Side effects such as sedation, slowed breathing, and reduced blood pressure are common when opiates are given orally or intravenously. However, sometimes, such as during childbirth, it is essential that the patient be alert, responding, and have healthy functioning of the respiratory and cardiovascular systems while at the same time being relieved of severe pain. To permit this, physicians often use a technique called **epidural analgesia**. With the patient lying on his or her side, a needle is carefully inserted between the vertebrae into the region immediately surrounding the spinal cord called the **epidural space**. Then, a small amount of opiate drug (such as fentanyl, morphine, or similar) is injected into the epidural space via a syringe connected to some plastic tubing (Figure 5.3). The opiate drug then binds to mu opiate receptors in the dorsal horn of the spinal cord and inhibits the activity

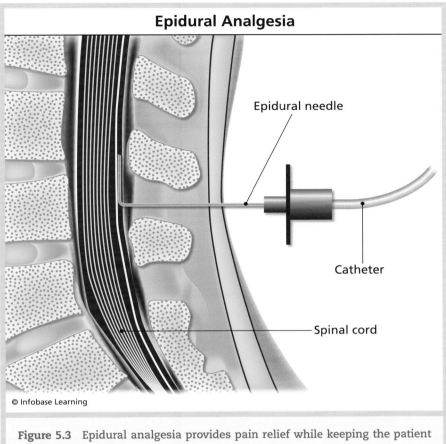

Epidural Analgesia

Epidural needle

Catheter

Spinal cord

© Infobase Learning

Figure 5.3 Epidural analgesia provides pain relief while keeping the patient alert and responsive.

of nerve cells that transmit pain signals to the brain. The injection is usually made in the lower back region, as this is where nerve fibers from the pelvic area enter the spinal cord. Because the drug remains confined to this small, localized area within the spinal cord, the patient feels no pain in the pelvic region, yet remains awake, alert, and responsive. When injected into the epidural space, the drug does not flow to the rest of the body, so the patient does not experience such side effects of opiates as nausea and vomiting. Finally, because less of the drug is needed during an epidural than would be for oral or intravenous administration, it takes less time for the drug to be eliminated from the body and thus results in a quicker recovery time.

There are, however, some mild side effects of epidural analgesia. The patient's legs often become numb and movement of the leg muscles is difficult. Other mild side effects include a backache (thought to be a result of over relaxation of the back muscles), itchiness in the skin, and the inability to urinate. Less commonly, patients may experience headache, lowered blood pressure, bleeding from the point of needle insertion, and patchy numbness (usually in the legs) that can last for up to three months after the epidural.

SUMMARY

Opiate drugs such as morphine are potent pain relievers that can be used to minimize the pain resulting from injury or numerous chronic pain conditions. Opiates inhibit the transmission of pain signals to the brain by binding to mu opiate receptors in the dorsal horn of the spinal cord, which inactivates the pain fibers and reduces the amount of pain signals being sent to the brain. There are numerous opiate pain relievers chemically related to morphine that have different potencies and durations of action. Unfortunately, long-term use of opiates to control chronic pain is hampered by the development of tolerance as well as physical dependence on opiates. Opiates are frequently used as epidural pain-relieving agents for childbirth procedures. Recent technological advances have allowed patients to deliver their own opiate pain relievers intravenously or as a nasal spray to better control their individual needs for pain relief.

6

Morphine Addiction

Marcus had been taking a single 10 milligram morphine pill every day for pain resulting from a neck injury he sustained during the last high school varsity football game of the season. Within a few weeks, the effectiveness of morphine in relieving his neck pain declined. He then asked his doctor to increase his dose of morphine, which the doctor did to 20 milligrams per day. A few weeks later, Marcus' neck pain was still bothering him, and he again asked his doctor to increase his dose. When his doctor refused, Marcus starting "double-dosing," taking two 20 milligram pills per day instead of one as his doctor had prescribed. Soon Marcus found himself experiencing a relentless preoccupation with obtaining more morphine. He made several appointments to see other doctors at nearby medical clinics with the intent of obtaining additional prescriptions for morphine, but each of these doctors declined because they had consulted with Marcus' primary doctor and knew he was already taking morphine for his injured neck.

Because he was so preoccupied with obtaining morphine, Marcus could not focus on his school work and his academic performance began to decline. With seemingly no other recourse to obtain morphine, Marcus broke into a local pharmacy late one night after they had closed and stole several bottles of morphine pills. Now with a substantial supply of morphine pills at hand, he began to take several morphine pills every 3 to 4 hours, and became so sedated that he could not stay awake during class or at home watching TV. One day his math teacher reported Marcus' repeated falling asleep in class to the school nurse, who then called

Marcus into her office and questioned him extensively until he revealed his heavy usage of morphine. Since Marcus was only 16 years old and not legally considered an adult, the school nurse immediately notified Marcus' parents, who searched Marcus' room and found his stash of morphine pills in his dresser drawer.

When Marcus returned home from school that day, his parents immediately took him to a drug rehabilitation facility for teenagers. Marcus was to stay at the facility 24 hours a day for 30 days. Approximately 36 hours after Marcus was admitted to the treatment facility, he began to experience symptoms of morphine withdrawal. These symptoms included watery eyes, sweating, diarrhea, and a severe headache. Recognizing that Marcus was a bona fide morphine addict undergoing withdrawal, the staff at the treatment facility prescribed him methadone to relieve these symptoms. With an hour of taking a methadone pill his withdrawal symptoms began to dissipate. Marcus remained at the treatment center for 30 days to overcome his addiction to morphine. Marcus never revealed any information about breaking into the pharmacy to anyone, and the robbery case was never solved by the local police.

Abuse of and addiction to morphine or other prescription pain relievers is a growing problem in the United States and many other countries. The number of prescriptions written for opiate pain relievers in the United States alone escalated from 40 million in 1991 to 180 million in 2007.[1] With specific reference to morphine, the number of prescriptions written increased from approximately 0.7 million in 1994 to almost 5 million in 2002, which is an increase of approximately 700 percent.[2] A similarly large (600 percent) increase in the use of opiates for treatment of pain has been documented in Denmark, and a smaller (89 percent) but significant increase in morphine prescriptions during approximately same time period has been observed in Australia.[3] Interestingly, however, between 2000 and 2008, the amount morphine consumed in Italy slightly decreased, whereas the consumed amount of oxycodone, fentanyl, and buprenorphine increased. The absence of an increase in morphine use in recent years in Italy may be a result of Italian physicians believing morphine is less safe than other opiate pain relievers.[4]

In parallel with the number of prescriptions written for narcotic pain relievers, the prevalence of their use in the United States and elsewhere has also dramatically increased since the 1990s. A 2008 survey conducted by the

U.S. National Institute on Drug Abuse found that among high school seniors, college students, and young adults, the prevalence (percent of these age groups) who had used prescription opiate pain relievers for nonmedical purposes was approximately 3 percent in 1991, and by the year 2007 this number had tripled to approximately 9 percent. This general increase in use and abuse of prescription opiate pain relievers, including morphine, is not merely a reflection of an increase in the number of people requiring pain medication for legitimate medical purposes, as there is substantial evidence that this increase in the number of prescription opiate users is paralleled by misuse of these drugs. This is evidenced by a similar increase in the number of emergency room visits related to prescription opiate misuse. Specifically regarding the misuse of morphine, U.S. government surveys showed that in 2004, the number of U.S. emergency department visits that were related to morphine misuse was approximately 14,000, and by 2006 this number had risen to more than 20,000. In addition, similar increases in the use, misuse, and overdose of other opiate pain relievers such as hydrocodone and oxycodone are being observed.[5] Before discussing the factors that contribute to the misuse/abuse of and addiction to morphine, a definition of drug abuse and addiction is needed.

DEFINITION OF DRUG ABUSE AND ADDICTION

The terms *drug abuse* or **substance abuse**, *drug dependence* or **substance dependence**, and **drug addiction** are often used interchangeably. However, the American Psychiatric Association's *Diagnostic and Statistical Manual of Mental Disorders, Fourth Edition* (DSM-IV) makes a clear distinction between the two official terms, substance abuse and substance dependence.[6] Substance abuse is a pattern of drug use that leads to impairments in social, occupational, or academic functioning and is demonstrated by one or more of the following occurring within a 12-month period:

- Repeated use of a substance resulting in impairments or inability to function socially, occupationally, or academically.
- Repeated use of a substance in physically hazardous situations (such as driving while intoxicated).
- Repeated use of a substance resulting in legal problems (such as arrests for illegally obtaining an opiate pain reliever without a prescription).

- Continued use of a substance despite its causing recurrent social or interpersonal problems.

Substance abuse almost always precedes the development of substance dependence, and the DSM-IV specifies that the two cannot occur in the same person at the same time.

Substance dependence—addiction—is a pattern of substance use that results in significant psychological and emotional distress, and impairment in a person's social, occupational, or academic functioning.[7] In order to meet the criteria for a diagnosis of substance dependence, a person must show at least three of the following symptoms or behaviors within a 12-month period:

- Tolerance to the effect of a given drug, characterized by increasing amounts of the drug being needed to produce the desired effect, or repeated taking of the same dose of the drug resulting in diminished psychological or physiological effects. In the case of opiate pain relievers, tolerance of the ability of these drugs to produce pain relief or feelings of well-being is common.
- The emergence of symptoms of withdrawal after discontinuing use of the drug. Many addictive drugs produce a cluster of withdrawal symptoms when a person who has repeatedly taken the drug suddenly stops taking it, and these symptoms can vary depending on the drug that was being used. Symptoms of withdrawal from chronic use of opiate pain relievers such as morphine (sometimes referred to as **opiate withdrawal syndrome**) usually begin 6 to 12 hours after the last dose was taken and peak two to four days after the drug use is stopped. Physical symptoms of opiate withdrawal include insomnia, restlessness, diarrhea, headache, nausea and vomiting, tremors, severe abdominal pain and cramping, body aches, increased blood pressure and heart rate (called **hypertension** and **tachycardia**, respectively), sweating, chills and goose bumps. Psychological symptoms of opiate withdrawal can persist for weeks or months long after the physical symptoms of withdrawal have subsided. These symptoms include depression, anxiety, mood swings, loss of appetite,

confusion, paranoia, and strong feelings of discomfort (often called **dysphoria**). Together, the physical and psychological symptoms of opiate withdrawal create intense desires and cravings for the opiate that person was previously using, which can drive the person to resume taking the drug so as to allievate the extreme discomfort of the withdrawal symptoms. Notice how many of the symptoms of opiate withdrawal are opposite to those produced by the drug itself—for example, dysphoria is the opposite of euphoria, diarrhea is the opposite of constipation, hypertension is the opposite of hypotension, and so forth.

- The drug is often taken in larger amounts or over a longer period of time than originally intended. For example, the 10 milligram dose of morphine should have adequately relieved Marcus' neck pain for about a week, but the body's necessity to constantly use the neck, even when lying down, made his neck problems persist and he continued to take the morphine for longer than originally anticipated.

- There is a persistent desire to cut down or abstain from using the drug, and attempts at reducing or stopping drug use are most often unsuccessful. The resumption of drug taking after trying to abstain is known as **relapse**, and is one of the primary problems that makes opiate addiction so difficult to treat effectively.

- A great deal of time is spent in trying to obtain, use, and recover from the effects of drug. For example, in our story of Marcus, he resorted to stealing morphine pills from the pharmacy in order to support his morphine habit.

- Drug use leads to reduced involvement in normal and important social, occupational, academic, or recreational activities. For example, Marcus' preoccupation with obtaining more morphine came at the expense of his school performance.

- The use of the drug is continued despite the user knowing that its use might lead to serious psychological, medical, legal, social, or financial problems. For example, despite knowing that his heavy use of morphine could potentially turn him into an addict, Marcus continued using morphine in larger doses and more frequently.

WHAT MAKES A PERSON START TAKING OPIATES? FACTORS CONTRIBUTING TO INITIATION OF PRESCRIPTION OPIATE USE

Since opiate narcotics such as morphine are pain relievers, most people begin taking them via a doctor's prescription instigated by a medical need for the drug, such as an injury or surgical procedure. However, some individuals start using prescription pain relievers out of curiosity and a desire for the feelings of relaxation and well-being that opiates produce. Without a medical need for the drug, these individuals can obtain morphine illegally via the Internet or sharing of "leftover" pills by friends who were taking an opiate for pain relief. In addition, younger individuals tend to be less educated about the addictive properties of opiates such as morphine.[8] Finally, people with easy access to opiate drugs, such as nurses, physicians, or anesthesiologists, often begin prescription opiate use out of the desire to "self-medicate" their own problems, whether they are psychological problems or for pain relief.

FACTORS CONTRIBUTING TO RECENT INCREASES IN PRESCRIPTION OPIATE ABUSE AND ADDICTION

Short-term users (a week or less of opiate use) rarely abuse or develop addiction to the drug.[9] So why has there been such a large increase in prescription use, abuse, and addiction to morphine and other opiate pain relievers in the past decade? There are numerous contributing factors, including increased access via the Internet, the development of formulations with prolonged effects which may increase the addictive nature of the drug, and a false sense of security held by medical professionals and hospital staff who believe that their medical training makes them less susceptible to opiate addiction than the "average" person. In fact, despite their formal training in medicine, opiate-abusing health care professionals have high rates of relapse and overdose even if they have undergone treatment for opiate addiction.[10]

WHAT CAUSES SOMEONE TO BECOME ADDICTED TO MORPHINE?

Addiction to any drug has long been viewed by society as a character flaw—a weakness or lack of willpower. However, the fact that some addictions tend to run in families, and that addictions are prevalent worldwide across many different cultures and ideologies, suggests that addiction may be more than just a psychological weakness. Most scientists now view addiction as being rooted, at least in part, in biology. The brain has its own **reward system**, which is primarily made up of neurons containing the neurotransmitter dopamine that send their axons throughout the brain; and when dopamine is released, feelings of pleasure and satisfaction occur.

It is currently believed that the brain's "reward" circuitry, which normally provides us with feelings of pleasure when we engage in behaviors that promote our survival such as eating, having sex, and having and caring for children, is also activated by addictive drugs. With repeated use, drugs such as morphine essentially "hijack" the brain's reward circuit, and skew our motivation to seek out stimulation by drugs rather than engage in normal rational behavior.[11] Research has shown that repeated use of morphine causes neurons to change the amount of certain proteins and chemical messengers that they produce, which has an overall effect of "rewiring" the brain. Even after a morphine addict has quit using the drug, his or her brain has been changed by the long-term morphine exposure, and the person is therefore likely to relapse due to his or her "rewired" brain.[12]

In addition to the ability of opiates to produce long-lasting changes in the brain, there are certain behaviors exhibited by opiate users that are predictive of whether or not the person will likely misuse or become addicted to the drug. Such behaviors that seem to indicate a person might become an opiate misuser or addict are selling their own prescription opiates to other people, forging prescriptions for opiates, stealing opiates, grinding up morphine or other opiate pills and injecting them intravenously, using alcohol or other illegal drugs in combination with opiate analgesics, increasing the dose of their medication numerous times, lying about having "lost" their prescription, seeking prescriptions for opiates from multiple doctors, and deterioration of family and other interpersonal relationships and performance at work.[13]

WHAT CAN LABORATORY RODENTS TELL US ABOUT THE ADDICTIVE NATURE OF DRUGS?

Scientists have used rodents as research subjects in many areas of psychology and medicine for more than a century. Although human beings often think of rats and mice as filthy, sewer-dwelling creatures, more than 90 percent of the genetic makeup of rats, mice, and humans is the same. As a result, medical experiments performed on rodents, as well as other nonhuman creatures such as guinea pigs, cats, dogs, and monkeys, have yielded valuable information about our biological makeup and have had a very important role in the development of new medicines, medical technologies, and approaches to the treatment of a vast number of diseases. Rodents have also provided a wealth of information on how addictive drugs change the brain. In tests for addiction potential, rats or mice are surgically implanted with catheters into one of their veins, and the catheter is connected to a pump that infuses a small amount of the drug (dissolved in a liquid solution) every time the animal presses a lever or performs some other task in a test cage. It turns out that rats and mice will repeatedly perform a task such as pressing a lever in order to receive numerous infusions of virtually every drug that is commonly abused by humans or is commonly addictive. Rats, mice, and other types of laboratory animals will perform specific tasks in order to receive intravenous infusions of morphine. Rats and mice will also continue to seek out morphine once it is taken away from them, and when rats are presented with stimuli (such as lights or sounds) that were present when the animal was initially taking the drug (and not when the rat was forced to be abstinent), they will resume pressing the lever that previously gave

OPIATE OVERDOSE

Some of the most frequently reported drugs on which people can overdose are opiate drugs, including morphine, heroin, methadone, buprenorphine, hydrocodone, and oxycodone. Approximately 4,000 deaths occurred in the United States in 2001 as a result of prescription opiate overdose, and this number more than doubled to over 8,000 by 2005.[14] Similarly, a recent survey conducted in them an infusion of morphine. This latter testing method is known as the "reinstatement" paradigm. It is commonly used for modeling relapse to drug addiction in humans, since people, places, or objects that addicts associate with drug use or the drug's effects (such as morphine-induced euphoria or pain relief) often trigger craving for the drug and causes the person to relapse. Interestingly, mice that have been genetically engineered so that their neurons cannot produce the the mu opiate receptor will not self-administer morphine when given the opportunity to do so, which indicates that this receptor is crucial for the pleasurable effects of the drug, even in rodents.[15]

Rodents can also help us understand some of the influences that the environment has on the desire to take drugs. For example, rodents are social creatures and like to live in groups. When a rat is placed in a cage by itself for a long period of time, this isolation becomes stressful. As is the case with humans, stress can increase the drive to "self-medicate" and take drugs to blunt one's psychological problems. A recent study examined the effects of social isolation on preference for morphine in rats.[16] In this study, laboratory rats were given two bottles on their cages, one containing water and the other with morphine diluted in the water. The researchers who conducted this study observed that rats housed alone (that is, socially isolated) drank more of the morphine-containing water than rats that were housed with another rat. When the isolated rat was allowed to interact with another rat for as little as an hour a day, its preference for the morphine-containing water decreased. These findings suggest that the stress of social isolation may cause lab rats to "self-medicate" themselves with morphine, and that social stresses may contribute to morphine use in humans as well.

England and Wales of opiate-related fatal overdoses showed that of five major illegal addictive drugs (heroin, cocaine, Ecstasy, amphetamine, and marijuana), heroin and morphine use has the highest mortality rate. In this survey it was revealed that the number of deaths where heroin or morphine was mentioned as the sole cause of death on the victims' death certificate was 481 in 2003, and by 2007 this number had grown to 587.[17] Together, these surveys indicate that the number of overdoses on morphine or heroin is steadily increasing.

Figure 6.1 Opiates such as morphine and heroin are among the most frequently documented causes of drug overdose. People who use opiates by intravenous injection are particularly vulnerable to fatal overdose. (© *Tek Image/ Photo Researchers, Inc.*)

High doses of opiates, taken as either large quantities of pills or by intravenous injection, can shut down the areas of the brain stem that control breathing, resulting in **fatal respiratory depression**. **Cardiac arrest** (stoppage of the heart) can also contribute to fatal overdose from opiates.[18] However, there is also evidence that opiate overdose is also associated with liver damage, especially in long-term opiate users, which suggests that in addition to increasing the risk of abuse and addiction, chronic use of opiates like morphine can actually damage the liver.[19]

SUMMARY

The use and misuse of morphine and other prescription opiate pain relievers has risen steadily in the United States during the past two decades. The number of fatal overdoses of morphine has also been increasing in recent years. People who are prescribed morphine for long-term use, such as those with chronic pain, have an increased risk of misusing or becoming addicted to morphine than people who are prescribed the drug for short-term use. Morphine addiction is characterized by tolerance to its pain-relieving and euphoria-producing effects, an extremely unpleasant withdrawal syndrome if the user stops taking morphine, taking the drug for longer periods of time or in greater quantities than originally intended, unsuccessful attempts at cutting down or stopping the use of the drug, spending increasing amounts of time obtaining, using, or recovering from morphine or its effects, and a significant impairment in daily functioning caused by use of the drug. Most morphine addicts initially take the drug for pain relief, although some people obtain it illegally solely for its pleasurable effects. Some health care professionals, such as nurses and anesthesiologists, are prone to abusing morphine or other opiates because they have access to the drug that is normally intended to be prescribed for patients. The pleasurable effects of morphine are believed to be mediated by its activation of the brain's reward circuitry, which causes the release of the neurotransmitter dopamine. In addition to producing addiction, chronic use of morphine leads to a rewiring of the brain and changes in the functioning of its neurons. Fatal overdoses from opiates, including morphine, are primarily due to respiratory depression.

7
Treatment of Addiction to Morphine and Other Opiates

Jess was a 28 year-old pharmacy intern who worked at a retail pharmacy chain. When his supervisor suddenly quit his job and left Jess to be the sole employee working the evening shift at the pharmacy, Jess felt as if he had unlimited access to hundreds of medications, and that if some went missing, no one would ever notice. Jess began secretly taking a few morphine pills out of bottles that were on the pharmacy shelf. After work, Jess would go home and take the morphine pills and enjoyably drift off to sleep while listening to his favorite music. Soon he found that the pills no longer produced the restful state of mind that he found so pleasurable, and he began stealing an increasing number of pills from the pharmacy. Eventually Jess found himself feeling very irritable and experienced chills in the early afternoon, so he started taking a few morphine pills prior to his work shift. This caused Jess to float in morphine-induced daze while working, and several times he dispensed the wrong medication for customers. When one customer returned to complain to the pharmacy manager about receiving the wrong medication, the manager went to question Jess and found him to appear sedated and "out of it". The manager immediately demanded that Jess take an over-the-counter urine drug test. At first Jess refused, but eventually he agreed to take the test. Not surprisingly Jess tested positive for narcotics. The manager then called the police and had Jess detained while he conducted an audit of all narcotic prescriptions filled at the pharmacy in the last month. The manager found that prescriptions for a total of

30 morphine pills had been received by the pharmacy, but that over 100 pills were unaccounted for.

The manager immediately pressed charges against Jess for illegal diversion of narcotics, and Jess was remanded to the local jail. A week later at his preliminary court hearing, Jess expressed deep sorrow for what he had done, and the judge took pity on him as a first-time offender and ordered Jess to pay a $1,000 fine and commit himself to an inpatient drug rehabilitation facility for 90 days. During the first part of his stay at the treatment facility, Jess was given low doses of methadone to curb his cravings for morphine. In addition, a Drug Enforcement Administration agent visited the facility and told him his pharmacy license was to be temporarily revoked. This frightened Jess, as his parents had invested a great deal of money in sending Jess to three years of pharmacy school, not to mention all the hard work Jess did while a pharmacy student. He also started to feel as if his future career as a pharmacist was suddenly ended, and he became very depressed. Jess then underwent psychological therapy at the facility to help with his feelings of depression, and to give Jess coping skills when his desire to use narcotic pills would occasionally surface. Jess met with his psychotherapist daily, and during the 90 days at the treatment facility he was also weaned off of the methadone so he could be drug-free and show no symptoms of opiate withdrawal. After being discharged from the rehab facility, Jess vowed to remain clean and felt as if he had been given a second chance at life. He took a job as a cashier at a supermarket while taking night classes to become re-certified to regain his pharmacy license.

Addiction to morphine or other prescription opiate pain relievers causes a great deal of personal, occupational, and medical complications. There is also a significant economic burden on society that results from addiction to prescription opiates, including lost productivity at the workplace, health and medical care costs, and legal and criminal justice expenses. It has been estimated that the costs of prescription opiate abuse in the United States total $8.6 billion annually, equivalent to approximately $16,000 per opiate abuser.[1] Of these individualized costs, approximately $7,600 is for treatment at a hospital or addiction treatment facility, $5,400 is for doctor visits, $2,000 is for the costs of the opiate medications alone, and the remaining costs are for miscellaneous expenses such as visits to other treatment facilities and emergency rooms.

There are two general approaches to treating addiction to opiate drugs, including morphine. The first is assisted detoxification followed by relapse prevention, and the other is opiate maintenance or replacement therapy.[2] These two approaches will be discussed below along with the steps that physicians can take to minimize the risk of the development of opiate addiction in their patients, as well as new treatments such as vaccine therapies.

ASSISTED DETOXIFICATION FOLLOWED BY RELAPSE PREVENTION

In this form of treatment for opiate addiction, the opiate addict is brought into a treatment facility and undergoes **detoxification**, in which they are forced to abstain (under medical supervision) from the use of any opiates for a period of 5 to 10 days in order to allow the body to rid itself of all traces of the opiate that was being abused. Normally, sudden stoppage of taking an opiate after having used it daily for many weeks or months would result in the severely unpleasant opiate withdrawal syndrome as discussed in Chapter 6. However, under medical supervision, the patient can be given various medications, such as clonidine, that reduce the severity of withdrawal symptoms.[3] In an effort to shorten the length of time it takes to detoxify an opiate addict, some physicians employ a technique called **rapid opiate detoxification**, in which the patient is administered an opiate receptor blocker (see below) to intentionally induce opiate withdrawal symptoms quickly as opposed to waiting for them to emerge hours after the patient last took his or her opiate drug. The symptoms of opiate withdrawal then dissipate over a shorter period of time (three to five days) as compared to the normal 5 to 10 days.[4] To further speed up the detoxification process, some addiction treatment specialists employ a technique called **ultrarapid opiate detoxification**, in which large doses of opiate receptor blockers are given to the patient while he or she is unconscious under general anesthesia. This allows the addict to undergo the opiate withdrawal process without being conscious and suffering the extreme discomfort of withdrawal symptoms.[5] Since this procedure involves a qualified anesthesiologist administering general anesthesia, which can lead to complications and even death in some individuals, it tends to be more costly and is used less frequently than standard or rapid opiate detoxi-fication procedures.[6]

However, medically assisted detoxification followed by relapse prevention tends to produce higher rates of relapse than opiate maintenance therapies (discussed below), primarily because prolonged use of the opiate "rewires" the addict's brain and makes him or her more prone to relapse.[7] In addition, when former opiate addicts do relapse, many times the result is a fatal overdose.

OPIATE MAINTENANCE AND REPLACEMENT THERAPIES

The most successful method to date for treating addiction to a prescription opiate pain reliever such as morphine is maintenance therapy (sometimes called replacement therapy). This method is similar to the nicotine patches that cigarette smokers use while trying to quit smoking: It allows them to avoid unpleasant withdrawal effects of having an addictive substance suddenly removed. Upon entering a treatment facility or seeing an addiction specialist, the opiate addict is no longer allowed to use his or her preferred opiate drug of choice (such as morphine or heroin), but instead is given a substitute opiate such as methadone (Dolophine), buprenorphine (Suboxone), or levo-alpha-acetylmethadol (LAAM).[8] In addition, drugs that inhibit the ability of opiates to activate the mu opiate receptor, such as naloxone or naltrexone, are also sometimes used.

Methadone

Methadone (Dolophine) was developed in the 1940s and introduced as a method for treating heroin addiction in the 1960s. Like morphine and other prescription opiates, methadone activates the mu opiate receptor. It has an average half-life of 24–36 hours, which allows for once-daily dosing, but in some individuals its half-life can be up to 150 hours. The most common unwanted side effects of methadone are sweating, constipation, and urinary retention. Although long-term methadone is not associated with toxic effects on the liver or kidneys, it is possible to overdose on methadone, particularly if it is combined with alcohol or sedatives such as sleeping pills. In addi-tion, methadone can cause some people to experience irregular heartbeats (**arrhythmia**). However, patients who are prone to developing arrhythmias

Figure 7.1 Methadone is often used to lessen the harsh symptoms of withdrawal during treatment for opioid addiction. (© Cordelia Molloy/ Photo Researchers, Inc.)

can usually be prescreened with the use of an **electrocardiogram**, which measures the electrical activity of the heart.

In the United States, dispensing methadone for the treatment of opiate addiction is restricted to government-certified federal and state facilities (commonly known as methadone clinics), and usually the patient has to visit the methadone clinic once daily to obtain his or her medication (that is, multiday or multiweek supplies of the drug are not given).[9]

Suboxone

In 2000, the U.S. Congress passed the Children's Health Act. This directed federal agencies to conduct long-term studies on children's health and development and how they related to diseases and conditions such as autism and asthma that some believe may result from exposure to harmful environmental factors. Title XXXV, Section 3502 of this act gave permission to properly trained physicians to treat opiate addiction, including children born to opiate-addicted mothers, with drugs that are approved by the Food and Drug Administration for such purposes, so that these treatments would be much more accessible and available than government-run methadone clinics. Then in 2002, the U.S. Food and Drug Administration approved the use of Suboxone for the treatment of opiate addiction. Like methadone, Suboxone is a long-acting drug with effects lasting up to 48 hours, allowing once-a-day dosing. It contains two types of opiates: buprenorphine, which activates the mu opiate receptor (although to a lesser degree than stronger opiates such as methadone, morphine, or oxycodone), and naloxone, which blocks the ability of opiates to activate mu opiate receptors. Suboxone was formulated in this manner to avoid potential abuse of this medication by addicts.[10] Normally, when Suboxone is taken in its proper form as a pill, the amount of naloxone in the drug formulation does not penetrate deeply into the bloodstream and is therefore relatively inactive. However, if the pills are used improperly, the naloxone directly enters the bloodstream and blocks the ability of any opiate to activate the mu opiate receptor. The end result would be the emergence of the unpleasant symptoms of opiate withdrawal.[11]

Levo-alpha-acetylmethadol (LAAM)

Levo-alpha-acetylmethadol (LAAM), also known as levacetylmethadol, levomethadyl, or its brand name Orlaam, is a synthetic derivative of methadone that, when taken orally in liquid form, is transformed into two active metabolites that activate the mu opiate receptor. The duration of action of these active metabolites is 48 to 72 hours, which allows it to be administered just three times per week. Like methadone and Suboxone, LAAM is effective as an opiate maintenance therapy.[12] However, as with methadone, some patients taking LAAM experience irregular heartbeats, and patients who are prone to develop this problem can usually be screened with the use of an electrocardiogram.

Opiate Receptor Antagonists

Another approach to treating opiate addiction is to give the addict a drug that blocks the ability of an addictive opiate such as morphine to interact with mu opiate receptors. Such drugs are called **opiate receptor blockers** or **opiate antagonists**. Two of the most widely used opiate antagonists are naloxone and naltrexone. Since these drugs block, rather than activate, mu opiate receptors, there is no potential for addicts to abuse or overdose on this drug. In addition, if while taking one of these drugs, the recovering addict has a relapse and resumes using opiates, their psychological and physiological effects will be blocked by the opiate antagonist. However, most evidence to date suggests that opiate antagonists do not have as great a success rate as methadone, buprenorphine, or LAAM in treating opiate addiction.[13]

PSYCHOTHERAPY AS AN AID IN THE TREATMENT OF OPIATE ADDICTION

Opiate maintenance therapies are often viewed as just "substituting one addictive drug for another," and some people feel they do not address some of the psychological issues that may be driving a patient's addiction to opiates. Behavioral counseling and interventions that appear to increase the success rates of opiate addiction treatment include:

- increasing the patient's motivation for undergoing treatment by providing positive feedback and setting realistic goals
- educating the addicts about the dangers of overdose and contracting diseases such as hepatitis C and HIV if they are abusing opiates intravenously
- **cognitive-behavioral therapy**, which teaches the addicts coping skills to help them deal more effectively with stress, resisting the urge to use drugs, identify factors that cause the addict to crave the drug, and teach the addicts what to do in case of a relapse.[14]

Group therapies such as Narcotics Anonymous (NA) can also help by providing a supportive network of peers to help patients overcome their addiction.

RESIDENTIAL TREATMENT FACILITIES VERSUS COMMUNITY SETTINGS

The ideal goal of an opiate addiction treatment program is complete abstinence from future opiate use and the prevention of relapse. However, the setting in which the treatment program takes place is often a critical indicator of whether or not the treatment will be successful. Overall, most studies have shown that residential treatment facilities—where those undergoing treatment (called inpatients) reside in the facility away from contact with family and friends for a period of one to three months or longer—seem to produce better rates of successful treatment than do community-based treatment programs, in which those in treatment (called outpatients) are allowed to live at home but must frequently visit their physician for observation to verify that they have not relapsed.[15]

ROLE OF PHYSICIANS AND PAIN SPECIALISTS IN MINIMIZING RISK FOR OPIATE ADDICTION

Because of the high rate of abuse and addiction to opiate pain relievers, many doctors are reluctant to prescribe them on a long-term basis, and have adopted strategies to minimize the chance of their patient developing opiate addiction. In addition, there is a growing consensus among doctors themselves, as people who have taken an oath to promoting the well-being of others, that they often play a role in the problem of prescription opiate addiction since they are the ones that authorize the prescriptions.[16] As mentioned earlier, some doctors, particularly those such as anesthesiologists who have access to opiate pain relievers, have a higher risk of opiate addiction than other types of physicians.[17]

Some doctors will first prescribe non-narcotic pain relievers (such as prescription strength acetaminophen or ibuprofen) to see if they can significantly relieve the patient's pain without resorting to opiates. Also, many doctors will closely monitor the patient's pain symptoms to determine if their degree of pain is declining over time, and compare that to the need for continued use of the opiate pain reliever. Other doctors utilize risk assessment procedures and scrutinize the patient's frequency of prescription refills, requests for dosage increases, and use of other drugs, and will ask the patient about work or their personal life to determine if any deterioration in social or occupational functioning has occurred. At the most stringent level, some doctors may ask their patients to undergo routine urine drug screens to determine if there are traces of any opiates (other than what may have been prescribed for treatment) present.

VACCINES FOR ADDICTION?

When we think of a vaccine, we normally think of a shot we receive at the doctor's office that will prevent us from contracting the flu, measles, polio, chickenpox, or other common diseases. Not many people think of addiction as something one might be vaccinated against. However, in the past decade there has been an increased effort in developing a vaccine (sometimes called an **immunotherapy**) to combat addiction. The idea behind a vaccine directed against an addictive drug is that if the immune system were properly stimulated with a vaccine, it would generate **antibodies** (small proteins produced by the body that target foreign molecules and flag them for destruction by the immune system) against a specific addictive-drug molecule, such as methamphetamine, heroin, morphine, or nicotine. The binding of the antibodies to the drug molecule would render it too large to be transported across the blood-brain barrier (discussed in Chapter 4), preventing it from having any type of effect on the central nervous system, such as producing euphoria.[18] Published studies on the effectiveness of such vaccines in humans are virtually absent since the idea is relatively new. However, there is evidence from studies in laboratory rats showing that a vaccine directed against the heroin and morphine molecules reduced the willingness of the rats to work for intravenous infusions of heroin.[19]

SUMMARY

Treatment of addiction to morphine and other opiates is typically approached by opiate maintenance therapy with the use of substitute drugs like methadone, Suboxone, or LAAM. Detoxifying opiate addicts is effective in eliminating addictive opiates from their bodies, but relapse rates without the use of maintenance drugs are relatively high. Psychological and behavioral counseling improves the success rates of treating opiate addicts with opiate maintenance, as does the use of residential treatment facilities. With increasing rates of prescription opiate analgesic abuse, physicians are beginning to take steps to reduce the incidence and risk of developing opiate addiction in patients who suffer from chronic pain and need to take opiates on a long-term basis. Finally, vaccines against opiates are being developed that prevent the penetration of the drug molecules into the brain, and are beginning to show potential as an aid in treating opiate addiction.

Appendix

Classification of Controlled Substances

In 1970, the U.S. government passed the Controlled Substances Act, which classified all drugs into one of five categories, or "schedules." In effect, this law classified drugs and other substances according to how medically useful, safe, and potentially addictive they are. These schedules are defined as follows:

> **Schedule I**—The drug has (1) a high potential for abuse, (2) no currently accepted medical use in the United States, and (3) a lack of accepted safety. Ecstasy is classified as a Schedule I substance, as are marijuana, heroin, psilocybin, LSD, and other hallucinogens such as peyote and mescaline.
>
> **Schedule II**—(1) The drug has a high potential for abuse, (2) the drug has a currently accepted medical use in the United States or a currently accepted medical use with severe restrictions, and (3) abuse of the drug may lead to severe psychological or physical dependence. Cocaine, morphine, oxycodone, hydrocodone, methamphetamine, and d-amphetamine are examples of Schedule II substances.
>
> **Schedule III**—(1) The drug has less potential for abuse than the drugs in schedules I and II, (2) the drug has a currently accepted medical use in treatment in the United States, and (3) abuse of the drug may lead to moderate or low physical dependence or high psychological dependence. Anabolic "body-building" steroids, ketamine, and many barbiturates are examples of Schedule III substances.
>
> **Schedule IV**—(1) The drug has a low potential for abuse relative to the drugs in Schedule III, (2) the drug has a currently accepted medical use in treatment in the United States, and (3) abuse of the drug may lead to limited physical dependence or psychological dependence relative to the drugs or other substances in Schedule III. Anti-anxiety drugs such as Valium and Xanax, as well as prescription

sleeping pills such as Ambien and Lunesta, are examples of Schedule IV substances.

Schedule V—(1) The drug has a low potential for abuse relative to the drugs or other substances in Schedule IV, (2) the drug has a currently accepted medical use in treatment in the United States, and (3) abuse of the drug may lead to limited physical dependence or psychological dependence relative to the drugs or other substances in Schedule IV. Certain narcotic-containing prescription cough medicines such as Motofen and antidiarrhea medicines such as Lomotil and Kapectolin PG are classified as Schedule V substances.

Notes

Chapter 1

1. M.J. Brownstein, "A Brief History of Opiates, Opioid Peptides, and Opioid Receptors," *Proceedings of the National Academy of Sciences USA* 90, 12 (1993): 5391–5393.
2. T.J. Maher and P. Chaiyakul, "Opioids (Bench)," in *Drugs for Pain,* ed. H.S. Smith (Philadelphia: Hanley & Belfus, 2003), 83–96; A. Aggrawal, *Narcotic Drugs* (New Delhi: National Book Trust, 1995).
3. Substance Abuse and Mental Health Administration, Results from the 2008 National Survey on Drug Use and Health: National Findings (Ed. NSDUH Series H-36). Office of Applied Studies, Rockville, MD, 2009.
4. P.M. Gahlinger, *Illegal Drugs: A Complete Guide to their History, Chemistry, Use and Abuse* (New York: Plume, 2004), 360.

Chapter 2

1. M.J. Brownstein, "A Brief History of Opiates, Opioid Peptides, and Opioid Receptors," *Proceedings of the National Academy of Sciences USA* 90, 12 (1993): 5391–5393.
2. Brownstein, "A Brief History of Opiates," 5391–5393; Gahlinger, *Illegal Drugs,* 19; L.D. Kapoor, *Opium Poppy: Botany, Chemistry and Pharmacology* (New York: Haworth Press, 1997), 2.
3. D.T. Courtwright, *Forces of Habit* (Boston: Harvard University Press, 2001), 151.
4. F.W. Sertürner, "Über die Entdeckung des Morphiums," *Journal von Pharmakologie (Leipzig)* 13 (1805): 29–32; F.W. Sertürner, "Darstellung der reinen Mohnsäure (Opiumsäure) nebst einer chemischen Untersuchung des Opiums," *Journal von Pharmakologie (Leipzig)* 14 (1806): 33–37.
5. J.D. Colliver and J.C. Gfroerer, "Motive for Nonmedical Use of Prescription Pain Relievers in the National Survey on Drug Use and Health," *Journal of Pain* 9, 6 (2008): 487–489, 494–496; S.E. McCabe, C.J. Boyd, J.A. Cranford, and C.J. Teter, "Motives for

Nonmedical Use of Prescription Opioids Among High School Seniors in the United States: Self-treatment and Beyond," *Archives of Pediatrics & Adolescent Medicine* 163, 8 (2009): 739–744; J.P. Zacny and S.A. Lichtor, "Nonmedical Use of Prescription Opioids: Motive and Ubiquity Issues," *Journal of Pain* 9, 6 (2008): 473–486; A.M. Gilson and P.G. Kreis, "The Burden of the Nonmedical Use of Prescription Opioid Analgesics," *Pain Medicine* 10 Suppl. 2, (2009): S89–S100.

6. L. Manchikanti, "National Drug Control Policy and Prescription Drug Abuse: Facts and Fallacies," *Pain Physician* 10, 3 (2007): 399–424; A.T. McLellan and B. Turner, "Prescription Opioids, Overdose Deaths, and Physician Responsibility," *Journal of the American Medical Association* 300, 22 (2008): 2672–2673.

7. Substance Abuse and Mental Health Administration, Drug Abuse Warning Network, 2006: National estimates of drug-related emergency department visits. Office of Applied Studies, Rockville, MD, 2008.

Chapter 3

1. T. De Quincey, *Confessions of an English Opium Eater*, ed. Alethea Hayter (New York: Penguin Books, 1971), 7.

2. L.D. Kapoor, *Opium Poppy: Botany, Chemistry and Pharmacology* (New York: Haworth Press, 1997), 7.

3. Ibid.

4. E. Kalso, "Oxycodone," *Journal of Pain and Symptom Management* 29, 5 Suppl. (2005): S47–S56; A. Murray and N.A. Hagen, "Hydromorphone," *Journal of Pain and Symptom Management* 29, 5 Suppl (2005): S57–S66.

5. D.W. Lachenmeier, C. Sproll, and F. Musshoff, "Poppy Seed Foods and Opiate Drug Testing—Where Are We Today?" *Therapeutic Drug Monitoring* 32, 1 (2010): 11–18.

6. G.B. Stefano, P. Cadet, R.M. Kream, and W. Zhu, "The Presence of Endogenous Morphine Signaling in Animals," *Neurochemical Research* 33, 10 (2008): 1933–1939.

7. Stefano, et al., "Presence of Endogenous Morphine," 1933–1939; M. Guarna, et al., "Neurotransmitter Role of Endogenous Morphine in CNS," *Medical Science Monitor* 11, 6 (2005): RA190–193; S.C. Pryor, et al., "Endogenous Morphine: Opening New Doors for the Treatment of Pain and Addiction," *Expert*

Opinion on Biological Therapy 5, 7 (2005): 893–906.

Chapter 4

1. R. Benyamin, et al., "Opioid Complications and Side Effects," *Pain Physician* 11, 2 Suppl (2008): S105–S120; C.E. Inturrisi, "Clinical Pharmacology of Opioids for Pain," *Clinical Journal of Pain* 18, 4 Suppl (2002): S3–S13.
2. Y. Zhang, Q. Chen, and L.C. Yu, "Morphine: A Protective or Destructive Role in Neurons?" *The Neuroscientist* 14, 6 (2008): 561–570.
3. M. Martin, R.A. Hurley, and K.H. Taber, "Is Opiate Addiction Associated with Longstanding Neurobiological Changes?" *Journal of Neuropsychiatry and Clinical Neurosciences* 19, 3 (2007): 242–248.
4. P. Sjogren, A.B. Thomsen, and A.K. Olsen, "Impaired Neuropsychological Performance in Chronic Nonmalignant Pain Patients Receiving Long-term Oral Opioid Therapy," *Journal of Pain and Symptom Management* 19, 2 (2000): 100–108; P. Sjogren, L.L. Christrup, M.A. Petersen and J. Hojsted, "Neuropsychological Assessment of Chronic Nonmalignant Pain Patients

Treated in a Multidisciplinary Pain Centre," *European Journal of Pain* 9, 4 (2005): 453–462.
5. See note 1 above.
6. Benyamin, et al., "Opioid Complications," S105–S120.
7. M. Alexander, T. Daniel, I.H. Chaudry, and M.G. Schwacha, "Opiate Analgesics Contribute to the Development of Post-injury Immunosuppression," *Journal of Surgical Research* 129, 1 (2005): 161–168; G.B. Stefano, G. Fricchione, Y. Goumon, and T. Esch, "Pain, Immunity, Opiate and Opioid Compounds and Health," *Medical Science Monitor* 11, 5 (2005): MS47–MS53.
8. J. Lotsch, "Opioid Metabolites," *Journal of Pain and Symptom Management* 29, 5 Suppl. (2005): S10–S24; G.K. Gourlay, "Advances in Opioid Pharmacology," *Support Care Cancer* 13, 3 (2005): 153–159.
9. J. Lotsch, "Opioid Metabolites," S10–24.

Chapter 5

1. C.E. Inturrisi, "Clinical Pharmacology of Opioids for Pain," *Clinical Journal of Pain* 18, 4 Suppl (2002): S3–S13; A. M.Trescot, S. Datta, M. Lee, and H. Hansen, "Opioid Pharmacology," *Pain Physician* 11, 2 Suppl. (2008): S133–S153.

2. B.M. Craig and S.A. Strassels, "Out-of-pocket Prices of Opioid Analgesics in the United States, 1999–2004," *Pain Medicine* 11, 2 (2010): 240–247.

3. K. A. Lehmann, "Recent Developments in Patient-controlled Analgesia," *Journal of Pain and Symptom Management* 29, 5 Suppl. (2005): S72–89.

4. Ibid.

5. A.M. Trescot, S. Datta, M. Lee, and H. Hansen, "Opioid Pharmacology," *Pain Physician* 11, 2 Suppl. (2008): S133–S153.

Chapter 6

1. Substance Abuse and Mental Health Administration, Results from the 2007 National Survey on Drug Use and Health: National Findings (NSDUH Series H-34). Office of Applied Studies, Rockville, MD, 2008.

2. W.M. Compton and N.D. Volkow, "Major Increases in Opioid Analgesic Abuse in the United States: Concerns and Strategies," *Drug and Alcohol Dependence* 81, 2 (2006): 103–107.

3. J. Hojsted and P. Sjogren, "An Update on the Role of Opioids in the Management of Chronic Pain of Nonmalignant Origin," *Current Opinion in Anaesthesiology* 20, 5 (2007): 451–455; L. Degenhardt, et al., "Trends in Morphine Prescriptions, Illicit Morphine Use and Associated Harms Among Regular Injecting Drug Users in Australia," *Drug and Alcohol Review* 25, 5 (2006): 403–412.

4. E. Bandieri, et al., "Prescription of Opioids in Italy: Everything but the Morphine," *Annals of Oncology* 20, 5 (2009): 961–962.

5. Substance Abuse and Mental Health Administration, Drug Abuse Warning Network, 2006: National estimates of drug-related emergency department visits. Office of Applied Studies, Rockville, MD, 2008; W.M. Compton and N.D. Volkow, "Major Increases in Opioid Analgesic Abuse in the United States: Concerns and Strategies," *Drug and Alcohol Dependence* 81, 2 (2006): 103–107; Centers for Disease Control and Prevention, "National Prescription Drug Threat Assessment 2009: Executive Summary," http://www.usdoj.gov/ndic/pubs33/33775/execsum.htm (accessed July 23, 2010).

6. American Psychiatric Association. *Diagnostic and Statistical Manual of Mental Disorders, 4th Edition, Text Revision.* (Washington, D.C.: American Psychiatric Press, 2002), 192–199.

7. W.M. Compton, and N.D. Volkow, "Abuse of Prescription Drugs and the Risk of Addiction," *Drug and Alcohol Dependence* 83, Suppl. 1 (2006): S4–S7.

8. Ibid.

9. J. Hojsted and P. Sjogren, "Addiction to Opioids in Chronic Pain Patients: A Literature Review," *European Journal of Pain* 11, 5 (2007): 490–518; W.M. Compton and N.D. Volkow, "Major Increases in Opioid Analgesic Abuse in the United States: Concerns and Strategies," *Drug and Alcohol Dependence* 81, 2 (2006): 103–107; W.M. Compton, and N.D. Volkow, "Abuse of Prescription Drugs and the Risk of Addiction," *Drug and Alcohol Dependence* 83, Suppl. 1 (2006): S4–S7.

10. W.M. Compton and N.D. Volkow, "Major Increases in Opioid Analgesic Abuse in the United States: Concerns and Strategies," *Drug and Alcohol Dependence* 81, 2 (2006): 103–107; K.H. Berge, M.D. Seppala, and W.L. Lanier, "The Anesthesiology Community's Approach to Opioid- and Anesthetic-abusing Personnel: Time to Change Course," *Anesthesiology* 109, 5 (2008): 762–764.

11. N.D. Volkow et al., "Dopamine in Drug Abuse and Addiction: Results of Imaging Studies and Treatment Implications," *Archives of Neurology* 64, 11 (2007): 1575–79.

12. R.M. Brown and A.J. Lawrence, "Neurochemistry Underlying Relapse to Opiate Seeking Behaviour," *Neurochemical Research* 34, 10 (2009): 1876–1887.

13. J. Hojsted and P. Sjogren, "Addiction to Opioids in Chronic Pain Patients: A Literature Review," *European Journal of Pain* 11, 5 (2007): 490–518.

14. Centers for Disease Control and Prevention, "National Prescription Drug Threat Assessment 2009: Executive Summary," http://www.usdoj.gov/ndic/pubs33/33775/execsum.htm (accessed July 23, 2010).

15. A. Becker, et al., "Morphine Self-administration in μ-opioid Receptor-deficient Mice," *Naunyn-Schmiedeberg's Archives of Pharmacology* 361, 6 (2000): 584–589; I. Sora, et al., "Mu Opiate Receptor Gene Dose Effects on Different Morphine Actions: Evidence for Differential In Vivo Mu Receptor Reserve," *Neuropsychopharmacology* 25, 1 (2001): 41–54.

16. S. Raz and B.D. Berger, "Social Isolation Increases Morphine Intake: Behavioral and Psychopharmacological Aspects," *Behavioural Pharmacology* 21, 1 (2010): 39–46.

17. L.A. King and J.M. Corkery, "An Index of Fatal Toxicity for Drugs of Misuse," *Human Psychopharmacology* 25, 2 (2010): 162–166.

18. J.M. White and R.J. Irvine, "Mechanisms of Fatal Opioid Overdose," *Addiction* 94, 7 (1999): 961–972.

19. S. Darke, S. Kaye, and J. Duflou, "Systemic Disease Among Cases of Fatal Opioid Toxicity," *Addiction* 101, 9 (2006): 1299–1305.

Chapter 7

1. S.A. Strassels, "Economic Burden of Prescription Opioid Misuse and Abuse," *Journal of Managed Care Pharmacy* 15, 7 (2009): 556–562; A.G. White, et al., "Direct Costs of Opioid Abuse in an Insured Population in the United States," *Journal of Managed Care Pharmacy* 11, 6 (2005): 469–479.

2. B. Jupp and A.J. Lawrence, "New Horizons for Therapeutics in Drug and Alcohol Abuse," *Pharmacology and Therapeutics* 125 (2010): 138–168.

3. Jupp and Lawrence, "New Horizons," 138–168; M.J. Krantz and P.S. Mehler, "Treating Opioid Dependence: Growing Implications for Primary Care," *Archives of Internal Medicine* 164, 3 (2004): 277–288.

4. M.J. Krantz and P.S. Mehler, "Treating Opioid Dependence: Growing Implications for Primary Care," *Archives of Internal Medicine* 164, 3 (2004): 277–288.

5. A.D. Kaye, et al., "Ultrarapid Opiate Detoxification: A Review," *Canadian Journal of Anesthesia* 50, 7 (2003): 663–671.

6. L. Gowing, R. Ali, and J. White, "Opioid Antagonists under Heavy Sedation or Anaesthesia for Opioid Withdrawal," *Cochrane Database of Systematic Reviews* 2 (2006): CD002022.

7. R.P. Mattick and W. Hall, "Are Detoxification Programmes Effective?" *Lancet* 347, 8994 (1996): 97–100; L. Amato, et al., "An Overview of Systematic Reviews of the Effectiveness of Opiate Maintenance Therapies: Available Evidence to Inform Clinical Practice and Research," *Journal of Substance Abuse Treatment* 28, 4 (2005): 321–329.

8. See note 3 above; L. Amato, et al., "An Overview of Systematic Reviews of the Effectiveness of Opiate Maintenance Therapies: Available Evidence to Inform Clinical Practice and Research," *Journal of Substance Abuse Treatment* 28, 4 (2005): 321–329; S. Ross and E. Peselow, "Pharmacotherapy of Addictive Disorders," *Clinical Neuropharmacology* 32, 5 (2009): 277–289.

9. S. Ross and E. Peselow, "Pharmacotherapy of Addictive Disorders," *Clinical Neuropharmacology* 32, 5 (2009): 277–289.

10. J.J. Manlandro, Jr., "Buprenorphine for Office-based Treatment of Patients with Opioid Addiction,"*Journal of the American Osteopathic Association* 105, 6 Suppl 3 (2005): S8–S13.

11. Ross and Peselow, "Pharmacotherapy," 277–289; Manlandro, "Buprenorphine," S8–S13.

12. Krantz and Mehler, "Treating Opioid Dependence," 277–288.

13. S. Minozzi, et al., "Oral Naltrexone Maintenance Treatment for Opioid Dependence," *Cochrane Database of Systematic Reviews* 1 (2006): CD001333.

14. M.M.Copenhaver, R.D. Bruce, and F.L. Altice, "Behavioral Counseling Content for Optimizing the Use of Buprenorphine for Treatment of Opioid Dependence in Community-based Settings: A Review of the Empirical Evidence," *American Journal of Drug and Alcohol Abuse* 33, 5 (2007): 643–654; L. Amato, et al., "Psychosocial and Pharmacological Treatments versus Pharmacological Treatments for Opioid Detoxification," *Cochrane Database of Systematic Reviews* 4 (2008): CD005031; L. Amato, et al., "Psychosocial Combined with Agonist Maintenance Treatments Versus Agonist Maintenance Treatments Alone for Treatment of Opioid Dependence," *Cochrane Database of Systematic Reviews* 4 (2008): CD004147.

15. M. Gossop, A. Johns, and L. Green, "Opiate Withdrawal: Inpatient Versus Outpatient Programmes and Preferred Versus Random Assignment to Treatment," *British Medical Journal (Clinical Research Edition)* 293, 6539 (1986): 103–104; E. Day, J. Ison, and J. Strang, "Inpatient Versus Other Settings for Detoxification for Opioid Dependence," *Cochrane Database of Systematic Reviews* 2 (2005): CD004580; M.J. Horspool,

N. Seivewright, C.J. Armitage, and N. Mathers, "Posttreatment Outcomes of Buprenorphine Detoxification in Community Settings: A Systematic Review." *European Addiction Research* 14, 4 (2008): 179–185.

16. S.D. Passik, "Issues in Long-term Opioid Therapy: Unmet Needs, Risks, and Solutions," *Mayo Clinic Proceedings* 84, 7 (2009): 593–601; R. Chou, "2009 Clinical Guidelines from the American Pain Society and the American Academy of Pain Medicine on the Use of Chronic Opioid Therapy in Chronic Noncancer Pain: What Are the Key Messages for Clinical Practice?" *Polskie Archiwum Medycyny Wewnetrznej* 119, 7–8 (2009): 469–477; S.D. Passik and P. Squire, "Current Risk Assessment and Management Paradigms: Snapshots in the Life of the Pain Specialist," *Pain Medicine* 10, Suppl. 2, (2009): S101–S114; K.H. Berge, M.D. Seppala, and A.M. Schipper, "Chemical Dependency and the Physician," *Mayo Clinic Proceedings* 84, 7 (2009): 625–631.

17. K.H. Berge, M.D. Seppala, and W.L. Lanier, "The Anesthesiology Community's Approach to Opioid- and Anesthetic-abusing Personnel: Time to Change Course," *Anesthesiology* 109, 5 (2008): 762–764; K.H. Berge, M.D. Seppala, and A.M. Schipper, "Chemical Dependency and the Physician," *Mayo Clinic Proceedings* 84, 7 (2009): 625–631; P. Sjogren, J. Hojsted, and J. Eriksen, "The Anaesthesiologist and Chronic Pain," *Acta Anaesthesiologica Scandinavica* 45, 9 (2001): 1057–1058.

18. B.M. Kinsey, D.C. Jackson, and F.M. Orson, "Anti-drug Vaccines to Treat Substance Abuse," *Immunology & Cell Biology* 87, 4 (2009): 309–314; B. Anton, et al., "Vaccines Against Morphine/Heroin and Its Use as Effective Medication for Preventing Relapse to Opiate Addictive Behaviors," *Human Vaccines* 5, 4 (2009): 214–229.

19. B. Anton and P. Leff, "A Novel Bivalent Morphine/Heroin Vaccine That Prevents Relapse to Heroin Addiction in Rodents," *Vaccine* 24, 16 (2006): 3232–3240.

Glossary

active metabolite   a molecule created by the metabolic breakdown of a drug or chemical substance that has significant biological activity

acute pain   pain that is relatively short-lived (seconds, minutes, hours, or days)

A-delta (A-δ) fiber   type of nerve fiber that transmits fast, sharp, localized pain

alkaline   having a basic (nonacidic and nonneutral) pH, typically 8 or above

alkaloid   a class of naturally occurring chemicals that contain nitrogen atoms and, when dissolved in water or other liquids, cause the solution to have an alkaline pH

ampule   small glass vial used for holding a drug solution

analgesia   a state of reduced or eliminated perception of pain

analgesic   a substance that provides relief from pain

anesthesia   a state of reduced perception of all sensations, including touch, pressure, pain, and temperature

antibodies   small molecules produced by the immune system that recognize specific foreign chemicals or organisms in the body

antitussive   having the ability to suppress the cough reflex

apothecary   older term for a pharmacist

arrhythmia   irregular heartbeat

axon   wire-like fiber of nerve cells that transmit electrical information

axon terminal   the end of an axon that contains chemicals used for communicating with other nerve cells

black tar opium   a form of opium that has an extremely thick and dark texture

bladder dysfunction   a disruption of proper functioning of the bladder

blood-brain barrier   the properties of blood vessels in the brain that allow fewer substances to pass out of the bloodstream into the surrounding tissue as compared with the rest of the body

cardiac arrest   stoppage of the beating of the heart

cell body   the main compartment of a nerve cell, which contains genetic material (DNA) as well as cellular "machinery" for making proteins

central nervous system (CNS)   portion of the nervous system composed of the brain and spinal cord

cerebral cortex   the outermost, wrinkled part of the brain that processes information and conducts higher-level brain functions such as thinking and planning

C-fiber   type of nerve fiber that transmits slow, dull, aching pain

chronic pain   pain that is long-lasting (weeks, months, or years)

cognitive-behavioral therapy (CBT)   a series of strategies aimed at correcting negative thought patterns and emotional responses in order to treat a psychological disorder such as drug addiction

constipation   decreased movement of digested food through the intestines

cross-tolerance   the development of tolerance to the effects of other drugs similar to the one currently used even though that particular drug may not have been previously taken

dendrite   branched fibers of nerve cells that receive information from other nerve cells

dependence   a state in which a person is chemically dependent on a drug, such that removal of the drug causes unpleasant withdrawal symptoms, and replacement of the drug alleviates the symptoms of withdrawal

detoxification   forced abstinence with the intent of allow the body to rid itself of an abused drug

dorsal horn   region where sensory nerve fibers, including those that transmit pain signals, enter the spinal cord

drowsiness   fatigue, sleepiness

drug abuse   *see* **substance abuse**

drug addiction   *see* **substance dependence**

drug dependence   *see* **substance dependence**

dysphoria   a state of discomfort or negative emotions such as irritability

electrocardiogram   a measure of the electrical activity of the heart

emesis   vomiting

endogenous   originating from within the body

endogenous morphine the actual morphine alkaloid chemical naturally produced by many animal species

epidural common name for the procedure of administering epidural analgesia

epidural analgesia relief from pain by injecting a pain reliever directly into the fluid surrounding the spinal cord

epidural space space between the vertebrae of the spine and the spinal cord that is filled with spinal fluid

euphoria a state of extreme pleasure, exhilaration, and sense of well-being

exogenous originating from outside the body

fatal respiratory depression stoppage of breathing resulting in death

fibromyalgia a medical condition commonly characterized by fatigue and widespread pain of unknown origin

half-life the time required for the body to metabolize or excrete half of a given amount of drug or other chemical substance

hemorrhoids painful, swollen veins in the lower portion of the rectum or anus

histamine a chemical released by cells of the immune system that causes the skin to itch

hyperalgesia a state in which a normally nonpainful sensation actually produces pain

hypertension blood pressure that is increased above the normal range

hypotension blood pressure that is reduced below the normal range

immunosuppression reduction in functioning of the immune system

immunotherapy a treatment for a disorder or disease based on altering the function of the immune system

interneuron a nerve cell that serves as an intermediate carrier of nerve impulses between two other nerve cells

latex in the context of opium harvesting, a synonym for opium

laudanum a liquid containing opium mixed with other mind-altering substances such as alcohol

M3G morphine-3-glucuronide; an inactive metabolite of morphine

M6G morphine-6-glucuronide; an active metabolite of morphine

maintenance therapy a type of therapy for drug addiction in which the addictive substance is replaced with a more benign substitute that prevents withdrawal symptoms and drug craving from emerging

malignant chronic pain pain that results from cancer

migraine   a severe and debilitating type of headache

miosis   reduction in the size of the pupil of the eye

mu (μ) opiate receptor (mu opioid receptor)   primary protein with which opiates such as morphine, as well as chemicals produced by the body such endorphins and enkephalins, interact

narcosis   a state of sleep, unconsciousness, or coma

narcotic   an opiate drug

nausea   a sensation of unease and discomfort in the stomach accompanied by an urge to vomit

neurons   nerve cells

neuropathy   damage to or malfunctioning of nerve endings

neurotransmitter   chemical messenger used by nerve cells to communicate with one another

nociception   the perception of pain

nociceptors   nerve endings that transmit the sense of pain

nonmalignant chronic pain   long-lasting pain that results from any medical condition other than cancer

nonmedical use   taking a drug for purposes other than its intended medical use, such as pleasure or euphoria

noxious   unpleasant, painful

nucleus   the part of the nerve cell body that contains genetic material (DNA)

opiate   a drug or substance derived from the opium poppy *Papaver somniferum*

opiate antagonist   a drug that prevents activation of an opiate receptor protein by an opiate drug

opiate receptor blocker   *see* **opiate antagonist**

opiate rotation   a procedure that attempts to circumvent tolerance to the pain-relieving properties of opiates by changing opiate medications frequently

opiate withdrawal syndrome   a set of symptoms experienced when use of an opiate drug after a prolonged period of time is suddenly stopped

opioid   pertaining to opiates, either from the opium poppy or similarly acting chemicals produced by the body

opium   a sticky, saplike substance that contains numerous pain-relieving and pleasure-producing chemicals, including morphine and codeine; also called **latex**

opium den   a house or room where people go to smoke or ingest opium for its pleasurable effects

osteoarthritis   joint pain caused by a progressive breakdown of the cushions of cartilage between bones in particular joints

patient-controlled analgesia (PCA)   a procedure in which a patient can inject himself or herself with pain-relieving medications

peripheral nervous system   portion of the nervous system outside the skull and spine that innervates the skin, muscle, and internal organs

phantom limb syndrome   physical sensations of the continued presence of an amputated limb, which can often be very painful

pneumonia   a potentially life-threatening infection of the lungs

pruritus   an itching sensation in the skin

psychomotor performance   manual dexterity, hand-eye coordination

pupillary constriction   reduction in the size of the pupil of the eye

rapid opiate detoxification   detoxification with the assistance of opiate receptor blockers

receptor   a protein that is designed to recognize a specific neurotransmitter molecule

relapse   resumption of taking a drug or drugs after a period of being abstinent

replacement therapy   *see* **maintenance therapy**

respiratory depression   a slowing of the rate or decrease in the depth of breathing, or complete stoppage of the act of breathing (*see* **fatal respiratory depression**)

reward system   the circuits of the brain that are activated when pleasurable events are experienced, either natural (food, sex, and the like) or by drug use

rheumatoid arthritis   joint pain caused by inflammation of the thin membranes lining the joints

sedation   fatigue, sleepiness

shingles   a medical condition characterized by damage to nerve endings in the skin that result from a reemergence of chickenpox virus particles from the spinal cord

side effects   often unpleasant symptoms experienced when taking a drug that occur in addition to the primary intended effect of the drug

sleep disturbance   a disruption in the amount of total sleep obtained or the amount of different stages of sleep

stupor   a state of heavy intoxication

substance abuse   a pattern of misuse of a drug that leads to decreased functioning in normal daily life, repeatedly using a drug in potentially hazardous situations, and repeatedly using a drug that results in legal, social or interpersonal complications; also called drug abuse

substance dependence   a prolonged pattern of drug use characterized by tolerance, withdrawal, repeated failed attempts to reduce or stop drug use, loss of normal daily functioning, taking drugs in larger quantities or for longer durations than originally intended, spending large amounts of time obtaining, using, or recovering from the effects of the drug, and continued drug use despite negative consequences; also frequently called drug dependence or drug addiction

synapse   a junction between two nerve cells where chemical messengers are used for communication

synaptic terminal   the end of an axon that contains chemicals used for communicating with other nerve cells

tachycardia   increased heart rate

thalamus   region of the brain where all sensory information passes through prior to entering the cerebral cortex

tolerance   reduced effectiveness of a drug due to repeated drug intake, which results in increasing the amount of drug taken to achieve the same desired effects as when the drug was first used

toxicity   the ability to cause healthy tissue or cells to become damaged or die

trigeminal neuralgia   acute but severe and recurrent facial pain

ultrarapid opiate detoxification   detoxification with the assistance of sedation by general anesthesia

urinary retention   decreased ability to urinate

vesicles   sphere-like storage compartments for neurotransmitters

withdrawal   unpleasant symptoms that are experienced when long-term use of a drug is suddenly stopped

Further Resources

Books and Articles

Davenport-Hines, R. *The Pursuit of Oblivion: A Social History of Drugs*. London: Phoenix/Orion Books, 2004.

Gahlinger, P. M. *Illegal Drugs: A Complete Guide to their History, Chemistry, Use and Abuse*. New York: Plume, 2004.

Smith, H. S. *Drugs for Pain*. Philadelphia: Hanley and Belfus, 2003.

Web Sites

Drug Addiction Support: Morphine Abuse Facts
http://www.drug-addiction-support.org/Morphine-Abuse-Facts.html

Drug Facts: Pain Killers
http://www.justthinktwice.com/drugfacts/painkillers.cfm

MorphineFacts.com
http://morphinefacts.com

Morphine Medical Facts from Drugs.com
http://www.drugs.com/mtm/morphine.html

Narcotics Anonymous
http://www.na.org

National Institute on Drug Abuse
http://www.nida.nih.gov

Partnership for a Drug-Free America
http://www.drugfree.org

Index

About the Author

M. Foster Olive received his bachelor's degree in psychology from the University of California, San Diego, and went on to receive his Ph.D. in neuroscience from UCLA. He was previously a member of the faculty of the Center for Drug and Alcohol Programs in the Department of Psychiatry and Behavioral Sciences at the Medical University of South Carolina. He is currently an assistant professor in the Behavioral Neuroscience division of the Department of Psychology at Arizona State University. His research focuses on the neurobiology of addiction, and he has published in numerous academic journals, including *Psychopharmacology, The Journal of Neuroscience*, and *Nature Neuroscience*. He has also authored several books in the series Drugs: The Straight Facts, including *Peyote and Mescaline, Sleep Aids, Designer Drugs, Crack*, and *LSD*, as well as *Ecstasy* in the Understanding Drugs series.

About the Consulting Editor

Consulting editor **David J. Triggle, Ph.D.,** is a SUNY Distinguished Professor and the University Professor at the State University of New York at Buffalo. These are the two highest academic ranks of the university. Professor Triggle received his education in the United Kingdom with a Ph.D. degree in chemistry at the University of Hull. Following post-doctoral fellowships at the University of Ottawa (Canada) and the University of London (United Kingdom) he assumed a position in the School of Pharmacy at the University at Buffalo. He served as chairman of the Department of Biochemical Pharmacology from 1971 to 1985 and as Dean of the School of Pharmacy from 1985 to 1995. From 1996 to 2001 he served as Dean of the Graduate School and from 1999 to 2001 was also the University Provost. He is currently the University Professor, in which capacity he teaches bioethics and science policy, and is president of the Center for Inquiry Institute, a think tank located in Amherst, New York and devoted to issues around the public understanding of science. In the latter respect he is a major contributor to the online M.Ed. program—"Science and The Public"—in the Graduate School of Education and The Center for Inquiry.